Network Culture

Network Culture

Politics for the Information Age

Tiziana Terranova

PlutoPress
www.plutobooks.com

First published 2004 by Pluto Press
345 Archway Road, London N6 5AA

www.plutobooks.com

Distributed in the United States of America exclusively by
Palgrave Macmillan, a division of St. Martin's Press LLC,
175 Fifth Avenue, New York, NY 10010

British Library Cataloguing in Publication Data
A catalogue record for this book is available from the British Library

ISBN   978 0 7453 1748 9 paperback

Library of Congress Cataloging in Publication Data
Terranova, Tiziana, 1967–
   Network culture : politics for the information age / Tiziana Terranova.
      p. cm.
   ISBN 0–7453–1749–9 (hb) — ISBN 0–7453–1748–0 (pb)
   1. Information society. 2. Information technology—Social aspects.
3. Information technology—Political aspects. I. Title. HM851.T47 2004
303.48'33—dc22

                                                                    2004004513

This book is printed on paper suitable for recycling and made from
fully managed and sustained forest sources. Logging, pulping and
manufacturing processes are expected to conform to the
environmental standards of the country of origin.

10 9 8 7 6 5 4

Designed and produced for Pluto Press by
Chase Publishing Services, Sidmouth, England
Typeset from disk by Stanford DTP Services, Northampton, England
Simultaneously printed digitally by CPI Antony Rowe, Chippenham, UK
and Edwards Bros in the United States of America

Contents

Acknowledgements

Many people, groups and institutions played a fundamental part in the writing of this book. The University of Berkeley's Engineering and Science Libraries (for their open doors policy of access and consultation); Danan Sudindranath, Mr Gary Pickens and Carol Wright for technical intelligence; the friends and former colleagues at the Department of Cultural and Innovation Studies, University of East London (and in particular Ash Sharma, Paul Gormley, and Jeremy Gilbert); the Signs of the Times collective; Martha Michailidou, Nicholas Thoburn and David Whittle (for reading and/or discussing parts of this work); Nick Couldry and the OUR MEDIA network; the ESRC, for funding part of this project; the Department of Sociology at the University of Essex (for granting two study leaves that allowed the writing of this book); Andrew Ross at the American Studies Centre, NYU, for his friendship and enduring support; Patricia Clough and the students at the CUNY Graduate Center for enthusiastic support and challenging feedback; the collective intelligences of *nettime*, *Rekombinant*, *Syndicate* and *e-laser* (for everything); Marco d'Eramo for his kind interest and bibliographical gems; the staff and students at the Center for Cultural Studies, Goldsmiths' College (Scott Lash and Axel Roch and for extra special support Sebastian Olma and Sandra Prienekenf); Riccardo and Simonetta; Betti Marenko from InSectCorp; the *Mute* collective (special thanks to Pauline van Mourik Broeckmann, Ben Seymour, Josephine Berry Slater, and Jamie King); my mentors and friends at the Istituto Universitario Orientale in Naples (especially Lidia Curti, Ian Chambers, Silvana Carotenuto and Anna Maria Morelli); the friends of the Hermeneia project at the Universitat Oberta de Barcelona (thanks to Laura Borràs Castanyer, Joan Elies Adell and Raffaele Pinto for some wonderful workshops); to Anne Beech and Judy Nash at Pluto Press, for their patience and for trusting their authors; Kode 9 from hyperdub.com and Daddy G from uncoded.net (for the bass lines and visions); and of course my family and friends back in Sicily, who provided free sunshine, blue sea, good food and warm company during the last stages in the writing of this book – the hot, hot summer of 2003.

Finally, special thanks to Luciana Parisi – for being a friend and a sister throughout our turbulent and co-symbiotic becomings.

To the Memory of
Vito Terranova
(1935–1992)

Introduction

This is a book about (among other things) information and entropy, cybernetics and thermodynamics, mailing lists and talk shows, the electronic Ummah and chaos theory, web rings and web logs, mobile robots, cellular automata and the New Economy, open-source programming and reality TV, masses and multitudes, communication management and information warfare, networked political movements, open architecture, image flows and the interplay of affects and meanings in the constitution of the common. It is a book, that is, about a cultural formation, a *network culture*, that seems to be characterized by an unprecedented *abundance* of informational output and by an *acceleration* of informational dynamics.

In this sense, this is a book about information overload in network societies and about how we might start to think our way through it. Because of this abundance and acceleration, the sheer overload that constitutes contemporary global culture, it was necessary to assemble and reinvent a method that was able to take in this bewildering variation without being overwhelmed by it. This method has privileged processes over structure and nonlinear processes over linear ones – and in doing so it has widely borrowed from physics and biology, computing and cybernetics but also from philosophy, and cultural and sociological thinking (from Baudrillard to Lucretius, from Deleuze and Guattari to Stuart Hall and Manuel Castells, from Michel Serres to Henri Bergson and Antonio Negri). Above all, however, this book is an attempt to give a name to, and further our understanding of, a global culture as it unfolds across a multiplicity of communication channels but within a single informational milieu.

To think of something like a 'network culture' at all, to dare to give one name to the heterogeneous assemblage that is contemporary global culture, is to try to think *simultaneously* the singular and the multiple, the common and the unique. When seen close up and in detail, contemporary culture (at all scales from the local to the global) appears as a kaleidoscope of differences and bewildering heterogeneity – each one of which would deserve individual and specific reflection. However, rather than presenting themselves to us as distinct fragments, each with its own identity and structure, they appear to us as a meshwork of overlapping cultural formations, of hybrid reinventions, cross-pollinations and singular variations. It is increasingly difficult to think of cultural formations as distinct entities because of our awareness of the increasing *interconnectedness* of our communication systems. It is not a matter of speculating about a future where 'our fridge will talk to our car and remind it to buy the milk on its way'. It is about an interconnection that is not necessarily technological. It is a tendency of informational flows to spill over from whatever network they are circulating in and hence to escape the narrowness of the channel and to open up to a larger milieu. What we used to call 'media messages' no longer flow from a sender to a receiver but spread and interact, mix and mutate within a singular (and yet differentiated) informational plane. Information bounces from channel to channel and from medium to medium; it changes form as it is decoded and recoded by local dynamics; it disappears or it propagates; it amplifies or inhibits the emergence of *commonalities* and *antagonisms*. Every cultural production or formation, any production of meaning, that is, is increasingly inseparable from the wider informational processes that determine the spread of images and words, sounds and affects across a hyperconnected planet.

Does that mean, as Paul Virilio has recently suggested following a prediction by Albert Einstein, that an unbearable catastrophe has struck the planet – that we are the victims, today, as we speak, of an informational explosion, a bomb as destructive as the atomic bomb?[1] Information is often described as a corrosive, even destructive and malicious entity threatening us with the final annihilation of space–time and the materiality of embodiment. Echoing a widespread feeling, Virilio suggests that we see information as a force able to subordinate all the different local durations to the over-determination of a single time and a single space that is also emptied of all real human interactions. From this perspective, contemporary culture is the site of a devastation wreaked by the deafening white noise of information, with its 'pollution of the distances and time stretches that hitherto allowed one to live in one place and to have a relationship with other people via face-to-face contact, and not through mediation in the form of teleconferencing or on-line shopping.'[2] As will become clear in the book, I do not believe that such informational dynamics simply expresses the coming hegemony of the 'immaterial' over the material. On the contrary, I believe that if there is an acceleration of history and an annihilation of distances within an informational milieu, it is a creative destruction, that is a *productive* movement that releases (rather than simply inhibits) social potentials for transformation. In this sense, a network culture is inseparable both from a kind of *network physics* (that is physical processes of differentiation and convergence, emergence and capture, openness and closure, and coding and overcoding) and a *network politics* (implying the existence of an active engagement with the dynamics of information flows).

The first chapter is a lengthy engagement with information theory with the stated intent of understanding more about this mysterious physical entity as it has come to pervade the language and practices of contemporary culture. I will start by freeing up the concept of information from two prejudices that have actually hindered our understanding of informational dynamics: the idea that information is 'the content of a communication'; and the notion that information is 'immaterial'. This interpretation of information theory (and in particular of Claude Shannon's 1948 paper on 'The Mathematical Theory of Communication') will play up those aspects of information that correspond to or explain the informational dynamics of contemporary culture (and hence the field of cultural politics). I have thus put forward a series of propositions linking information theory to something that we call 'the cultural politics of information' and have tried to understand how such a shift has transformed and affected the cultural politics of representation (both linguistic and political). The relationship between physical concepts such as entropy and negentropy, noise and signal, micro and macro, nonlinearity and indeterminacy determines the production of a 'materialistic' theory of information that could help us to make better sense of the 'chaos of communication' in which we live.

The second chapter discusses the architecture of networks, and more specifically the architecture of the Internet. In this case, the Internet is taken as a technical diagram able to support the development of an informational space that is driven by the biophysical tendencies of open systems (such as the tendency towards divergences, incompatibilities, and rising entropic levels of randomness and disorganization). Here I take the Internet to be not simply a specific medium but a kind of active implementation of a design technique able to deal with the openness of systems. The design of the Internet (and its technical protocols) prefigured the constitution of a neo-imperial electronic space, whose main feature is an openness which is also a constitutive tendency to *expansion*. The chapter explores how the informational dynamics instantiated by the design philosophy of the Internet is actualized in a series of topological figures and cultural experimentation in phenomena such as blogging, mailing lists, and web rings.

Chapter three is an investigation into the question of the 'digital economy' or the 'New Economy' (as it has become more commonly known). In particular, the chapter looks at the phenomenon of 'free labour' – that is the tendency of users to become actively involved in the production of content and software for the Internet. The difficulties inherent in the relationship between such forms of volunteer and unpaid technocultural production and our understanding of contemporary capitalism will be a central focus of the chapter. In order to understand this relation I will draw on the Marxist notion of 'real subsumption' of society under capitalism. In particular, I will follow the Autonomist Marxist suggestion that the extension of production to the totality of a social system (the 'social factory' thesis) is related to the emergence of a 'general intellect' and 'mass intellectuality' pointing to capital's incapacity to absorb the creative powers of labour that it has effectively unleashed.

Chapter four is devoted to the problem of 'control' in chaotic and self-organizing systems – a leitmotif of early literature on the Internet and a field of intense controversy between the human and natural sciences. Recent developments in biological computation (such as research on artificial life, neural networks and mobile robots) imply the production of a kind of 'technical diagram' of control that takes as its content the autonomous productive capacities of a large number of interacting variables. Such a diagram entails the interconnection of the many; the decentralization of command; the modulation of local rules and global behavior; and a kind of 'unnatural selection' in the form of predesigned aims and objectives that operate to capture the powers of emergence through the reconstitution of individuality. The chapter suggests that the dynamics of flows – once understood in terms of nonlinear relations between a larger number of simple bodies – is far from constituting a utopian state of pre-Oedipal bliss but has become the field of operation of a new mode of cybernetic control (or soft control).

Finally chapter five looks at the implications of such distributed and internetworked informational milieus for our understanding of the political dimension of communication. Is it still possible to talk of the media as a 'public sphere' in an age of mass propaganda, media oligopoly and information warfare? Is the world splitting between an educated and internetworked public opinion and a passive and manipulated mass of TV junkies? The chapter suggests that a reappropriation of the properties of the 'mass' (or the implications of 'forming a mass') can help us to untangle the semantic properties of communication (the meaningful statements that it transmits) from its intensive, affective ones. If the mass is a field for the propagation of affects, it does not exclude but *includes* and *envelops* within itself the segmentation of specialized audiences and their further microsegmentation over the Internet. This common milieu, interconnected by the flow of images and affects, is the site for the emergence of new political modes of engagement (such as Internet-organized global movements against neoliberal economic policies and the Iraqi war). The chapter concludes by proposing such network culture as a site of the political constitution of the common through the biopower of communication.

Throughout this book, I have tried to find a way to map these transformations, not simply as *technologies* but also as *concepts, techniques and milieus*. These are concepts that have opened up a specific perception and comprehension of physical and social processes; techniques that have drawn on such concepts to develop a better control and organization of such processes; and milieus that have dynamically complicated the smooth operationality of such techniques. In no case have I noticed a linear relation of cause and effect between technologies and social change, or, for that matter, between concepts, techniques, processes and milieus.

From another perspective, I also have to warn the reader that I have willingly overemphasized the dimension of communication and information over other aspects of social and cultural change. In no way should this be taken as an indication of an alleged obsolescence of other aspects of contemporary culture or politics. This overemphasis works in this book as a kind of methodological device to temporarily isolate a specific type of process for the purposes of analysis. In particular, the exceptional dynamism of such informational milieus might lead one to overlook the persistence of stratifications and structures across the domains observed. On the other hand, it is this dynamic character that has drawn my attention to the subject and kept our interest throughout this project and I cannot but hope my readers will feel the same.

1
Three Propositions on Informational Cultures

Is there an informational quality that defines twenty-first century culture – a quality that makes such culture unique, that gives it, so to speak, its most characteristic and peculiar trait? Such a question would appear to be based on two problematic assumptions: in the first place that there is something like *a culture* that defines a century; and, above all, that we do know what such informational quality is about – that is, that we do know the 'meaning of information'.

If the notion of *a culture* raises important questions about the relationship between the heterogeneous and the homogeneous, the idea that we do not know what information is might appear as less of an issue. After all, information has become such a common word and is used so freely and with such ease that we should have no problem at all in defining it. We know at least two things about information: that it is the content of a communication act; and that there is something less than material about it – at least judging from the ease with which it goes from mouth to ear and ear to mouth. This immateriality of information has been further amplified by technical developments that have made possible the instant transmittal and multiple distribution of any type of information at all (images, sound, music, words, software, statistics, projections, etc.). It is this ease of copying, it has been argued, that makes of information such a shifty and yet valuable commodity. We know that information can be sold and bought and that a good deal of the world economy is driven by an emphasis on the informational content of specific commodities and we are also aware that information itself can be valuable (when it is used for example to make a profit in the stock market). We know that anybody is always potentially an information-source or even an information-storage device and that science suggests that information constitutes the very basis of our biological existence (in as much as, we are told, we contain information that can be decoded within our very cells). In all these cases, information emerges as a

6

content, as some kind of 'thing' or 'object' but one that possesses abnormal properties (ease of copying and propagation, intangibility, volatility, etc.) that contemporary technological developments have exacerbated and amplified.

These features of the informational commodity have opened all kinds of issues around the question of *rights* in the digital age – and more specifically the right to own and copy information. Thus we have a political struggle around the right to keep medical information private; the right not to have one's personal correspondence or data monitored and/or sold; the right to copy and distribute music and video over the Internet; the right to make low-cost copies of patented medications in cases of national health emergencies (such as the AIDS epidemics in Africa); and the right to profit from information that has been produced at great cost to the producer. In all these cases, however, information is still treated as a content of a communication – a content to be protected whether in the interests of individuals, institutions, companies or the commonwealth at large. Surely, if there is a political struggle around information at all, then it must be about issues such as copyright and intellectual property. As far as the rest of contemporary culture is concerned, surely it must be business as usual – with the usual conglomerates and political parties trying to manipulate media representations for their own hegemonic purposes.

And yet, useful and important as such struggles are, they do not really address for us the larger problem of the relation between 'culture' and 'information'. Information, that is, might be more than simply the content of a communication. We are no longer mostly dealing with information that is transmitted from a source to a receiver, but increasingly also with informational dynamics – that is with the relation between noise and signal, including fluctuations and microvariations, entropic emergencies and negentropic emergences, positive feedback and chaotic processes. If there is an informational quality to contemporary culture, then it might be not so much because we exchange more information than before, or even because we buy, sell or copy informational commodities, but because cultural processes are taking on the attributes of information – they are increasingly grasped and conceived in terms of their informational dynamics.

It is thus important to remember that, as a historical concept pointing to the definition, measurement, analysis and control of a mathematical function, information does not coincide with the rise of a digital media system. On the contrary, the appearance of information theory parallels the emergence and development of modern mass media such as telegraphy, telephony, radio and television. Unlike previous media such as print and writing, modern media, in fact, do not use the code of a workaday language, but 'make use of physical processes which are faster than human perception and are only susceptible of formulation in the code of modern mathematics'.[1] We could refer to the informatization of culture as starting with the analogue function of *frequency*, that is with the encoding of sound in the grooves of a gramophone record, where speech phonemes and musical intervals were recognized for the first time as complex frequency mixtures open to further mathematical analysis and manipulation.[2] For Friedrich Kittler, it is also with telegraphy that information, in the form of massless flows of electromagnetic waves, is abstracted for the first time. In this sense, information is not simply the content of a message, or the main form assumed by the commodity in late capitalist economies, but also another name for the increasing visibility and importance of such 'massless flows' as they become the *environment* within which contemporary culture unfolds. In this sense, we can refer to informational cultures as involving the explicit constitution of an *informational* milieu – a milieu composed of dynamic and shifting relations between such 'massless flows'.

And yet, one could suggest that these massless flows are far from being immaterial (or at least not in the sense in which the term is used, that is in the sense of something that is not quite of this world). An assessment of the informational dynamics of culture forces us to confront/address the analytical and political categories informing our understanding of cultural politics and its relation to the informational quality identified above. In the English-speaking world in particular, the last 30 years have seen a predominant focus on analytical categories such as meaning, identities and representation opening up onto a cultural politics of *identity, representation,* and *difference.* The question of media and communications has thus been related mainly to the problem of how a hegemonic consensus emerges out of the articulation of diverse interests; and how cultural struggle is waged within a representational space, marked by the relationship between self and other, or the identical and the different. The political dimension of culture has thus been conceived mainly in terms of *resistance to dominant meanings;* and the set of tactics opened up have been those related to the field of representation and identity/difference (oppositional decodings; alternative media; multiple identities; new modes of representation).

The emergence of informational dynamics has thus caught the more militant strands of media and cultural theory as if by surprise. Information is no longer simply the first level of signification, but the milieu which supports and encloses the production of meaning. There is no meaning, not so much *without* information, but *outside* of an informational milieu that exceeds and undermines the domain of meaning from all sides. Unless we want to resign ourselves to the notion that culture has been made immaterial and transcendent by an informational deluge, we need to reassess the ways in which we understand the relationship between culture, power, and communication. What is proposed here is that an engagement with information theory is rich in analytical insights into the features of contemporary cultural politics where such informational dynamics are increasingly foregrounded. In particular, it allows us to move away from an exclusive focus on meaning and representation as the only political dimension of culture. In as much as communication is not simply the site of the *reproduction* of culture, but also that of an indeterminate production crossing the entirety of the social (from factories to offices to homes and leisure spaces), it also constitutes a kind of common informational milieu – open to the transformative potential of the political.

Keeping these questions in mind, in this chapter we will focus on the 'meaning' of information. In particular, I will turn to information theory (and specifically the early work of Claude E. Shannon and the cyberneticians) to catch the points where information ceases to be simply the content of communication and gains, so to speak, a body – that is a materiality in its connection with the world of physics, engineering and biology. I will thus isolate three definitions of information as related by Shannon's 1948 paper: information is defined by the relation of signal to noise; information is a statistical measure of the uncertainty or entropy of a system; information implies a nonlinear and nondeterministic relationship between the microscopic and the macroscopic levels of a physical system. These hypotheses are the basis out of which Shannon built his mathematical definition of information, but they also offer some other interesting considerations or *corollaries* on informational cultures. These corollaries suggest that within informational cultures, communication is crucially concerned with the problem of noise and contact; that the cultural politics of information are not only about privacy, property and copyright, but also open up the question of the *virtual,* that is the relation between the given and the (allegedly) unlikely; that information flows displace the question of linguistic representation and cultural identity from the centre of cultural struggle in favour of a problematic of mutations and movement within immersive and multidimensional informational topologies.

INFORMATION AND NOISE

The fundamental problem of communication is that of reproducing at one point either exactly or approximately a message selected at another point.[3]

Proposition I: Information is what stands out from noise
Corollary Ia: Within informational cultures, the struggle over meanings is subordinated to that over 'media effects'
Corollary Ib: The cultural politics of information involves a return to the minimum conditions of communication (the relation of signal to noise and the problem of making contact)

As elaborated by the researchers working for telecommunication companies in the first half of the twentieth century, information theory is fundamentally concerned with the accurate reproduction of an encoded signal. The reproduction of information is at the heart of the communication process in as much as the latter fundamentally involves the accurate reproduction of a pattern from a sender to a receiver through a channel. If such information is transmitted accurately, that is with minimum distortion and corruption, then the communication act can be said to have been successful. If the information is distorted or does not reach its destination, then the communication act has been unsuccessful. The new techniques of communication management are crucially concerned with the relation between signal and noise with the explicit intent of generating a 'media effect'. The nature of such media effects, however, needs to be reconsidered within the larger context of an 'informational milieu'.

In order to better understand the implication of introducing an informational perspective into our evaluation of culture, we need to engage with information theory in more detail. The modern scientific concept of information has a mixed and hybrid genealogy, at the crossing of science and engineering, involving a cross-disciplinary dialogue between physics, mathematics, biology and even sociology (in its positivistic, 'social physics' version). A rigorous mathematical theory of information, however, was developed only in the 1940s by members of the cybernetic group and by engineers at AT&T's Bell Laboratories (and in particular by R.V.L. Hartley, Harry Nyquist, and Claude E. Shannon). For Jérôme Segal, the milieu of communication engineers working in corporate labs in the United States was particularly rife for such technical and scientific breakthroughs. On the one hand, the US engineers did not share the narrow vocational focus that kept their European peers within the social hierarchy of a theory/practice divide. North American telecommunication engineers had been trained in physics departments (for example, on MIT's *Electrical Engineering* course) and had thus a good knowledge of the most abstract and complex physics debates.[4]

On the other hand, US communication engineers were also confronted by complex problems of speed and accuracy in signals transmission posed by the large telecommunication networks of the United States, where signals had to be repeatedly relayed before reaching their destinations. It would also be hard to underestimate the importance of the internationalization and interdisciplinarization of science during and immediately after World War II – a process that provided the material circumstances for the constitution of a theory of information linking physics, statistics and telecommunications and that prepared the ground for the informatization of life in molecular biology. The concept of information was part of research taking place within the field of 'communication and control engineering' – a branch of engineering that depended on a larger theory of messages involving the contribution of linguistics and cryptoanalysis to the understanding of communication codes. Norbert Wiener went so far as to argue that the difference between the older field of power engineering and communication engineering marked a shift from the long nineteenth century of the industrial society to a new cybernetic age of communication, command, and control.[5]

Shannon established his reputation as the pivotal point around which a century of attempts to conceptualize information as a physical quantity revolved on the basis of a paper on what he called 'the mathematical theory of communication', published in the *Bell System Technical Journal* in 1948. Shannon's paper advanced a set of theorems that dealt 'with the problem of sending messages from one place to another quickly, economically, and efficiently'.[6] Shannon's 'Mathematical Theory of Communication' was republished by the University of Illinois Press in 1949, together with Warren Weaver's less mathematically oriented paper. As a result, the mathematical theory of communication is often referred to as the Shannon–Weaver model – a ground-breaking effort in the field of communication engineering and a necessary reference in all attempts to tackle some of the implications inherent in an informational understanding of communication. The modern concept of information is explicitly subordinated to the technical demands of communication engineering, and more specifically to the problems of the 'line' or 'channel'. Shannon's definition of information is dependent on the problematic of the accurate reproduction of a weak impulse or signal across a range of different media channels (telegraphy, telephony, radio, television, computing). Information is thus described through a mathematical function that could be used to maximize the transmission of a signal through a channel. His logarithmic measure of information is still fundamental to the 'design of every modern communications device – from cellular phones to modems to compact-disc players.'[7]

The problem identified by researchers at the Bell Laboratories is well known to all communication engineers and high fidelity sound enthusiasts. When a signal travels through a channel, it often produces a characteristic background static that is not solved by amplification. In this sense, the signal is always identified in relation to what threatens to corrupt and distort it, that is noise. Communication engineers identified the noise in channels with the discrete character of the electrons carrying the current. Amplification did not correct the disturbance because messages or signals ended up swamped by their own energy.[8] The problem could not be solved simply by increasing or decreasing the amount of energy flowing through a channel, but various types of filters proved to be a partially effective solution. What was needed, however, was a technique to encode the signal in such a way that it would minimize loss of quality by some kind of error-control instructions. Engineers thus needed a function that would enable them to build systems that could distinguish noise from signal and hence correct the corruption of messages. But in which ways is a signal mathematically distinguishable from noise? This question required a method for identifying information as an entity that could be separated from the meaning that could be made of it. For Claude E. Shannon, messages '[f]requently ... have *meaning;* that is they refer to or are correlated according to some system with certain physical or conceptual entities. These semantic aspects of communication are irrelevant to the engineering problem'.[9] From the point of view of information theory, 'two messages, one of which is heavily loaded with meaning and the other of which is pure nonsense, can be exactly equivalent...'[10]

In order to frame his concept of information properly, Shannon drew his famous diagram that, beyond becoming indispensable to the technical development of communication and information technologies, was also to have substantial repercussions for the emerging fields of mass communication research and media and cultural studies. Shannon's diagram identified five moments or components in the communication process: an information source, a transmitter, the message, the channel of communications and the receiver. It is a deceptively simple diagram. The information source, or sender, selects a message to be coded into a signal that is then transmitted through a channel to a receiver. Information is the content of communication, in the sense that it is what needs to be transported with the minimum loss of quality, from the sender to a receiver (as if in an older mode of communication when the latter mainly referred to physical transport). At the same time, this content is not defined by its meaning, but by a mathematical function – a pattern of redundancy and frequency that allows a communication machine to distinguish it from noise. As all information theorists will emphasize, although we can attribute meanings to information, the latter does not coincide with its meaning. An encoded television signal or a piece of software has no meaning in the conventional sense.

Information, that is, is far from simply constituting a kind of degree zero of code, in the sense of a basic, denotative level of meaning. The postmodern lesson on the cultural politics of information is that meaning has evaporated as the main point of reference within the scene of communication. Or, in a different way, information can be understood to involve a larger spectrum than meaning, as F. J. Crasson suggested when he compared information to phenomenological understandings of perception where 'the meaningful is related to the continuous fulfillment of expectations and is opposed therefore (by Husserl) to heterogeneous discontinuity or (by Merleau-Ponty) to complete homogeneity'.[11] Meaningful experiences thus disappear

at each end, as it were, of the information spectrum, both its maximal and minimal points. In terms of its meaninglessness, maximal randomness in the visual field is hardy distinguishable from minimal randomness. Information is thus a term of far greater extension than meaning.[12]

From an informational perspective, a meaningful perception, one that can be made sense of and articulated, is a statistical compound of the familiar and the unfamiliar. It is both redundant and random; we grasp it because it is partially new and partially familiar. Thus Crasson draws the conclusion that meaning is 'what makes sense, produces no surprises, requires a minimal amount of information to define its shape'.[13] Indeed, Crasson (like Jean Baudrillard 20 years later) will conclude that information and meaning might be inversely proportional: the more information the less meaning. In this sense, the proliferation of information spells the drowning of meaningful experiences in a sea of random noise. In an informational culture the middle zone of meaning is increasingly difficult to construct and maintain, in as much as the noise always implicitly carried by information hedges in from all sides. In this sense, an informational culture marks the point where meaningful experiences are under siege, continuously undermined by a proliferation of signs that have no reference, only statistical patterns of frequency, redundancy and resonance (the obsessive frequency and redundancy of an advertising campaign, the mutually reinforcing resonance of self-help manuals and expert advice, the incessant bombardment of signifying influences). Holding on to the 'message' in order to drown the noise of contrasting information is what allows the stability necessary in order to establish a contact. But in this case, what stops information from being just another name for brainwashing? And does that imply that the scene of communication, the cultural politics of information as such, is exclusively a theatre of manipulation favouring the expertise and concentrated knowledge of a new breed of communication managers? If information identifies an operationality of communication strategies, spreading out from military technology to civil society at large, isn't it another name for communication as a sophisticated form of mind control?

There is no doubt that the manipulation of affects and signs is an essential part of the politics of communication in informational cultures. What is more difficult to uphold, however, is the behaviourist perspective that identifies the influence of the media with that of a simple command in a drastic simplification of the physical dynamics of communication as such. Information theory, thus, highlights the minimum conditions for communication, and thus attributes a *secondary* importance to the question of the *meaning* of messages when compared to the basic problem of *how to increase the effectiveness of the channel*. Information can be anything: a sound, an image, a colour, and of course also words. The problem of communication is reduced to that of establishing a bridge or a contact between a sender and a receiver. The two extremities of the channel 'are on the same side, tied together by a mutual interest: they battle together against noise'.[14] Resistance to communication is not related to misinterpretation or dissent, but to an inhuman interference (what Michel Serres calls the 'demon of noise'). The scene of communication is reduced to its minimum condition: that of making contact by clearing a channel from the threat of noise.

This conception of communication is well suited to the technical demands of the channel within modern media such as telephony, radio and television, where the integrity of the signal is always potentially undermined by the distortion of noise. At the same time, however, this does not really imply the ultimate influence of a technological determination, but more a return to the minimum condition of communication as such. The minimum condition for communication (in the animal and the machine, as Wiener put it) is contact – a temporary suspension of the multitude of tiny and obscure perceptions out of which information emerges as a kind of fleeting clarity, as if a space had been successfully cleared. It does not matter who the sender or receiver are, whether they are machines, animals, bacteria, genetic sequences, or human organisms. Reason and meaning, dialectics and persuasion, truth and falsehood are all temporarily evacuated from the scene. There is no longer an interlocutor or an audience to address, there is no rhetorical play of ideas, but a kind of bare set, where all communication is reduced to a drive to clear out a channel for transmission between two points separated by space and united only by the channel. From an informational perspective, communication is neither a rational argument nor an antagonistic experience based on the capacity of a speaker to convince a listener or to impose his perspective. The information flow establishes a contact between sender and receiver by excluding all interference, that is by holding off noise. Interlocutors are not opposed, as in the traditional conception of the dialectical game, but they are *assumed* to be on the same side. Opposition to the agreement between sender and receiver cannot be subjective, but only objective and external, appearing only in the non-human form of meaningless *noise* (or the form of an enemy intent on disrupting the communication between two partners in agreement). *'To hold a dialogue is to suppose a third man and to seek to exclude him.'*[15]

The appearance of a modern informational problematic, then, is related to a conception of communication as an operational problem dominated by the imperatives of the channel and the code rather than by a concern with exchange of ideas, ethical truth or rhetorical confrontation (a definition that dominates the liberal and enlightened concept of communication). It is not about signs, but about signals.

This technical (rather than simply technological) conception of communication is what for us opposes, for example, the ethics of modern professionals of communication (such as journalists) to today's communication managers (PR agents, advertisers, perception managers, information strategists, directors of communication). While journalists who subscribe to a professional ethics rooted in a liberal modernity, for example, would argue that information must be assessed in terms of its accuracy (or truth value) and relevance (meaningfulness), communication managers seem to have another type of grasp of the informational dimension of contemporary culture – which they reduce to a Manichean battle between signal and noise. The latter, in fact, understand the power of a communication act as determined by the overall dynamics of the informational milieu, where what counts is the preservation of the message/signal through all the different permutations and possible corruptions which such a message/signal is liable to undergo. This is why, for example, this social management of communication favours the short slogan or even the iconic power of the logo. The first condition of a successful communication becomes that of reducing all meaning to information – that is to a signal that can be successfully replicated across a varied communication milieu with minimum alterations. Whether it is about the Nike swoosh or war propaganda, what matters is the endurance of the information to be communicated, its power to survive *as information* all possible corruption by noise.

When a television debate is held, for example, between competing politicians in the wake of an election, can we say that such a debate is won or lost on the basis of a dialectical argument involving the interplay of truth and persuasion? Can we say that politicians are really conveying a persuasive content? Or isn't the main problem that of clearing out a channel through a noisy mediascape, of establishing a contact with the audience out there? In this context, the opponent becomes noise and the public becomes a target of communication: not a rational ensemble of free thinking individuals, endowed with reason, who must be persuaded, but a collective receiver to which a message can be sent only on condition that the channel is kept free of noise (competing politicians, but also the whole noisy communication environment to which such politicians relate, where, for example, more young people vote for reality TV shows than for general elections). Or in another context: don't the techniques of advertising involve, first of all, an attempt to bypass the noise of a crowded informational milieu by establishing a connection with potential customers? The purpose of communication (the exclusion of noise and the establishment of contact) is simultaneously presupposed, technically produced, and actively reinforced. It is understandable, then, why cultural activism of the *No Logo* variety should have focused so much on what Mark Dery has called 'culture jamming' – signal distortion, graffiti on advertising posters, hijacking of corporate events, all kind of attempts at disrupting the smooth efficiency of the communication machine. Or, as Gilles Deleuze suggested, why cultural resistance within control societies might also involve the creation of 'vacuoles' of non-communication able to elude the latter's command. Or why, in conditions of media monopoly, the problem becomes that of undermining the stronghold of such tyrannical contact by opening up as many other venues of communication as possible (from festivals to the Internet, from demos and workshops to screenings, dancing and public performances).

The conditions within which a cultural politics of information unfolds are thus those of a communicational environment that has been *technically* reduced to its 'fundamental problem', as Shannon put it (or its minimum conditions as we would say). It is such minimum conditions that must be recreated each time by the techniques of communication: the successful constitution of a contact, the suspension of all competing signals and the filtering out of all possible corruption of the message in transit. There is nothing inherently technological here, in the modern sense of a Frankenstein monster which has been created by human will but which is now threatening to destroy it. It is not so much a question of technology as of techniques and forms of knowledge that all converge – through a variety of media and channels – on the basic problem of how to clear out a space and establish a successful contact.

Does that mean, then, that journalists and activists who hang on to relevance and truth and meaning have been made redundant by communication managers with a much better grasp of informational dynamics? The problem here is not that of arguing for the obsolescence of meaning and truth in favour of sheer manipulation within an informational milieu. It might be the case, that is, that such managers and entrepreneurs might have themselves misunderstood the informational dimension of communication as such and that their repeated efforts at amplifying the signal in order to drown out the noise might be as counterproductive in a social sense as they would be within the circuit of a stereo system. As ARPANET directors J. C. R. Licklider and Robert W. Taylor will later put it, such theory is based on the unsatisfactory assumption that communication is simply about two people now knowing what only one knew before (the name of a brand; the central message of a political speech).[16] The tactics of amplification, the attempt to control the scene of communication by sheer power, might backfire because it does not take sufficiently into account the powers of *feedback* or retro-action – increasingly cynical or even angry audience/receivers or just a kind of social entropy that nonlinearizes the transmission of messages as such.

In this sense, the critique made by Gilbert Simondon of the technical theory of communication (as he called the work of telecoms engineers) opens up an interesting perspective on the dynamics of communication beyond meaning but also beyond the operational demands of the channel. For Simondon, the mathematical theory of communication underestimated information by reducing it to what is transmitted between two distinct and individuated extremities: a sender and a receiver. The relation of communication for Simondon does not take place between two preconstituted individuals (such as a politician and his audience, for example), but between the pre-individual (what within the formed individual resists individuation) and the collective (the dimension within which another type of individuation takes place). Both the sender and the receiver, the politician or his director of communication and their audience, are in fact immersed within a larger field of interactions that packs within itself a constitutive potential that the mathematical theory of communication does not capture. All communication always involves a metastable milieu, characterized by an incompatibility among different dimensions of a pre-individual and collective being. Information is thus not so much the content of communication, as one of its dimensions, and more specifically it indicates the direction of a dynamic transformation. For Simondon, information theorists underestimated the conditions of turbulence and metastability that define information as a kind of active line marking a quantic process of individuation.[17] What this comes down to, in relation to our understanding of the cultural politics of information, is that the act of establishing a contact might not be reduceable to a kind of informational command – where the ultimate target is the control of what audiences think and feel. On the contrary, the informational dimension of communication seems to imply an unfolding process of material constitution that neither the liberal ethics of journalism nor the cynicism of public relations officers really address.

For example, in some ways the informational dimension of communication seems to implicate a production of reality in a way that does not only involve our capacity to signify – that is, to know the world through a system of signs. In as much as information concerns the problem of form it also poses the question of the organization of perception and the production of bodily habits which it foregrounds with relation to the emergence of social meanings. Within design and architecture, for example, information is also about the active transformation of bodily habits as this takes place around keyboards and chairs, games, trains and cars, buildings and small objects with which we perform all kind of daily actions. Information is not about brainwashing as a form of *media effect*, but it does also involve a level of *distracted* perception; it thus informs habits and percepts and regulates the speed of a body by plugging it into a field of action. In this sense, the informational dimension of communication is not just about the successful delivery of a coded signal but also about contact and tactility, about architecture and design implying a dynamic modulation of material and social energies. Information works with forms of distracted perception by modulating the organization of a physical environment.[18] This active power of information is everywhere: it is in the interfaces that relay machines to machines and machines to humans; it is in material objects including chairs, cars, keyboards, and musical instruments. It is in bottles and telephones in as much as they lend themselves in a particular way to the action of a hand. It is not an essence, understood here as a transcendent form, but it indicates the material organization of a possible action that moulds and remoulds the social field. The return of communication to its minimum conditions makes the whole field of culture and society (not simply the media) open to the informational redesign and hence, to the action of a code. A cultural politics of information, as it lives through and addresses the centrality of information transmission, processing and communication techniques, opens up a heightened awareness of the importance of minute and apparently inconsequential decisions as they are implemented in architecture and design, on television and the Internet, in medical research and news-making, in personal relationships and working practices. In this sense, the relation of signal to noise with which we have opened our understanding of information and which dominates the perspective of the social engineering of communication does not exhaust the informational dimension of culture as such. As we shall see, in fact, this dimension is concerned not only with the successful transmission of messages, but also with the overall constitution of fields of possibilities – of alternatives and potentials that are transforming the problem of *representation* as cultural theory has come to think of it.

THE LIMITS OF POSSIBILITY

Suppose we have a set of possible events whose probabilities of occurrence are $p1$; $p2$; ...; pn. These probabilities are known but that is all we know concerning which event will occur. Can we find a measure of how much 'choice' is involved in the selection of the event or of how uncertain we are of the outcome?[19]

Proposition II: The transmission of information implies the communication and exclusion of probable alternatives.
Corollary II: Informational cultures challenge the coincidence of the real with the possible.

Information theory understands all codes as operating within statistical constraints that make the succession of symbols more or less likely (which allows the maximization of information transmission through a channel). Another key implication, however, is that all events (from the occurrence of a symbol within a code to all communication acts) can be described as a selection among a set of mutually excluding and more or less probable alternatives. The communication of information thus implies the reduction of material processes to a closed system defined by the relation between the actual selection (the real) and the field of probabilities that it defines (the statistically probable). The relation between the real and the probable, however, also evokes the spectre of the improbable, the fluctuation and hence the virtual. As such, a cultural politics of information somehow resists the confinement of social change to a closed set of mutually excluding and predetermined alternatives; and deploys an active engagement with the transformative potential of the virtual (that which is beyond measure)

The breakthrough that gave Shannon's paper such relevance outside the circles of telecom engineers was a little parenthesis that he opens up in the middle of his paper on the mathematical theory of communication, entitled 'Choice, uncertainty, entropy'. As he somewhat self-deprecatorily explained,

> This theorem, and the assumptions required for its proof, are in no way necessary for the present theory. It is given chiefly to lend a certain plausibility to some of our later definitions. The real justification of these definitions, however, will reside in their implications.[20]

In this section, he identified information as a measure of the probabilities of occurrence of an event (including the choice of one symbol over another within a code) – and hence a single selection among possible states. This measure was provided for him by statistical mechanics – a discipline that tackled thermodynamic processes through the tools of statistics. As we will see, the nineteenth-century physicist Ludwig Boltzmann identified the entropy of a closed system (that is, the tendency of such a system to lose structure while also running out of useful energy), with an uncertainty in our knowledge of the system. For thermodynamics, all irreversible processes involve the interaction of a large number of particles that can be distributed in a variable number of states. Because of the numbers involved, we cannot really know such systems in detail. All we can have is a statistical description that allows us to calculate the *probabilities of occurrence of events*. Not an absolute and determinate description (as in classical physics), but a probabilistic evaluation of the states in which a system might be.

Shannon's breakthrough was to apply such a statistical understanding of entropy to the theory of messages or information theory. 'Entropy is a probability distribution, assigning various probabilities to a set of possible messages. But entropy is also a measure of what the person receiving the message *does not know* about it before it arrives.'[21] Shannon applied this statistical understanding of sets of messages to the problem of 'code'. In particular, he looked at language as a code and observed that codes such as the English language obeyed definite statistical laws that determined the likely frequency of any combination of letters (there is a higher probability that c will be followed by h than by z, for example). The English language was thus defined as a code that involved approximately 50 per cent individual freedom in the choice of symbols and 50 per cent necessity as established by the statistical laws of the code. By mathematizing the relationship between redundancy and freedom in a code such as English, one could devise some means to encode the message more effectively. The 'choice' of the individual speaker is constrained by the statistical laws of language.

Warren Weaver, among others, drew from such theory a key consequence. Such definition of information implied that the action of a code on a situation was also a kind of *containment* of the openness of the situation to a set of mutually excluding alternatives. The code predetermines, and it does so statistically. 'The concept of information applies not to individual messages (as the concept of meaning would), but rather to the situation as a whole ... *Choices are, at least from the point of view of the communication system, governed by probabilities ...'*[22] For Norbert Wiener, 'the transmission of information is impossible save as a transmission of alternatives. If only one contingency is to be transmitted, then it may be sent most efficiently and with the least trouble by sending no message at all.' Hence, it is convenient for transmission and storage purposes, to consider a unit amount of information as 'a single decision between equally probable alternatives'.[23] Each transmitted unit of information is thus a *selection* (hence Shannon's theory is also referred to sometimes as the *selective* theory of information).

Let us look at a concrete example of such a selective and statistical conception of information as given by another cybernetician, W. Ross Ashby.[24] A man has committed a crime and been arrested. He does not know whether his partner in crime has been arrested or not. His wife must communicate to him an essential piece of missing information (whether or not his confederate has been caught by the police). The only communication allowed between her and her husband is a cup of tea (in this case the channel); she will either put sugar in the tea or not depending on whether the confederate has been caught or not (this is her code); the jailer can also be expected to try to interfere in the communication if he can (he is the noise). There is here a priori information (the crime–jail scenario); a degree of uncertainty in this system (as determined by two probable states: the confederate has either been caught or not); a sender and a receiver (the wife and husband); a channel (cup of tea); a code (presence/absence of sugar); an interference (the jailer).

This situation and its uncertainty can thus be measured on the basis of a statistical distribution of probabilities. In this case, there are two alternative or probable states given to the information source (or wife): the confederate has either been caught or not. The field constituted by the husband, the wife, the prison, the prison guards, the cup of tea, the confederate, and the police gives rise to a closed set of messages. The confederate might have got away with it or might have been caught; hence the uncertainty of the situation can be expressed through a simple binary code (yes or no), that is one bit (or binary digit). However, the information source or sender (the wife) is limited in the information that she can send by the channel (there is not much information that you can communicate through a cup of tea). Because the only transaction that is allowed between herself and her husband is a cup of tea, then the latter is the channel and the capacity of such a channel will put constraints on the coding of the uncertainty of the situation. For example, they might agree that sweetened tea would be a yes and unsweetened would be a no.

Of course, communication also includes the possibility of a corruption of the message in transit by noise. The jailer might have figured out that the tea can be used as a means of communication and he might interfere by telling the prisoner that he had sweetened it himself. If the wife wanted to make sure that the message got through, she would thus need some way of inserting some redundancy into the code, thus doubling the probability of the information surviving the noise (she might have agreed also to add or not to add milk, for example). Although the code might be different, both cases are equally likely, so the amount of information that needs to be transmitted is ultimately low (a choice between two possibilities expressible by way of a single bit). What the example illustrates is the principle that, as Warren Weaver put it, 'the unit information indicates that in this situation one has an amount of freedom of choice, in selecting a message, which is convenient to regard as a standard unit amount.'[25] The measure of the information that is produced when the message is chosen from the set is the amount that the woman can communicate to her jailed husband. This amount of information can be reduced to the logarithm of the probabilities of the situation and thus be prepared for communication through a suitable channel. The value of information theory for cybernetics, according to Ross Ashby, lies exactly in its representing a given situation as a set of mutually excluding alternatives. It does not ask what individual answer it can produce, but 'what are *all* the possible behaviours that it can produce' and how likely one behaviour is when compared to another. The value of information theory is that it deals with such sets of probabilities.

This example challenges us to think about information in ways that are markedly different from the commonsensical ways in which we have come to regard it – not simply as content but also as a kind of representation of a reality out there. Communication theory explicitly states that information involves the reduction of both a set of messages and a milieu of interaction to their statistical properties. Information thus operates as a form of probabilistic *containment* and *resolution* of the instability, uncertainty and virtuality of a process. It is thus implicated in a process by which alternatives are reduced and the uncertainty of processes is prepared for codification by a channel. Uncertainty can be measured and solved by applying a set of constraints to a situation that unfolds into a binary mode of 'either/or'. 'The transmission of information is impossible save as a transmission of alternatives.'[26] Within the mathematical theory of communication, information represents an uncertain and probabilistic milieu by reducing it to sets of alternatives that determine more or less likely sets of possibilities on the basis of a given distribution of probabilities as determined by the relation between channel and code.

What the communication of information implies, then, is not so much a relation between the 'real' and its 'copy' (or its representation), but the reduction of a process to a set of probabilities. It still holds true, that is, that information does not only address the dimension of interpretation or meaning (even though it also carries meaning and it is also subject to interpretation). But this operation of signification is secondary with relation to a primary operation which is that of the reduction of a situation to a set of more or less probable states and alternatives as constrained by the interplay between a channel and a code; and the reduction of communication to the resolution of such uncertainties through the selection of one of the alternatives from the set (this selection does not necessarily involve a human subject, but can be spontaneously generated). In this sense, for many critics of information and communication theory, the latter are almost exclusively modes of power involved in the reproduction of a system.[27] The communication of information related, for example, to a new deal between a government and a trade union, adds to our knowledge of the situation only in as much as that situation has been reduced to a set of possible outcomes (deal/no deal; strike/ negotiations) that can be easily encoded within the medium of the news. The communication of information about a possible war similarly reduces the complexity of a situation to a set of pre-closed alternatives. Nothing new is really added, only some (im)probable alternatives eliminated (such as other modes of knowledge or methods of analysis).

The transmission of information concerns alternatives formulated on the basis of known probabilities within the constraints set up by the interplay of code and channel or medium. That is why the most effective and concise modality of information transmission today is that of the opinion poll, the survey, risk assessment and all other types of information that can be easily encoded for survival in the meta-medium of an informational milieu. What is the probability that I will develop a fatal disease if I keep smoking? How is the popularity of the government doing today? How many points did the Dow Jones lose today and what are the chances that it will go up? Is it by chance that there is a whole sector of the financial markets, such as that of futures, that is based on a kind of legal gamble on the probable future? Whether it is marketing research, polls-informed public policy, or medical decisions, the transmission of information involves the action of a code and a channel setting the limits within which the problem can be presented and mapping out sets of possible alternatives. The political technology of information societies is crucially concerned with the organization of the field of the probable or the likely. It thus produces a sensibility to social change (and forms of subjectivity) that are informed by the relation between the real and the possible – where the real is what remains while all other competing possibilities are excluded.

Once again what we are presented with here is not simply the effect of a technological organization of communication, but a set of relays between the technical and the social. The closure of the horizon of radical transformations that is implied in the probabilistic nature of information and the code is not simply the effect of information and communication technologies. On the contrary, it is once again a matter of techniques and impersonal strategies as they distribute themselves on the macroscopic consensus about the ultimate triumph of the existent. A cultural politics of information thus also implies a renewed and intense struggle around the definition of the limits and alternatives that identify the potential for change and transformation. The cultural politics of information, as it unfolds across the distributed networks of communication, often involves a direct questioning of the codes and channels that generate the distribution of probabilities – that is the production of alternatives as such. It is exactly because all information assumes the constitution of a closed field of possibilities that the cultural politics of information is often centrally directed to constraints and 'lack of choice' as is. A cultural politics of information is crucially concerned with questioning the relationship between the probable, the possible and the real. It involves the opening up of the virtuality of the world by positing not simply different, but radically other codes and channels for expressing and giving expression to an undetermined potential for change.

Even as mediated by the space of statistical probability, in fact, the relationship between the real and the probable that is enacted within the informational dimension of communication does not ontologically exclude the possibility of the extremely improbable (or of the *virtual*). As Marco d'Eramo has put it, the probability of a system's being in a certain state is not a property of its being. Probabilities do not exclude the possibility of a fluctuation that violates the organized space of the real and the possible.

> If we say that water boils at 100 degrees Celsius, we are really saying something else: that, at 100 degrees in a pot, water has a very high chance of boiling, but, at the same time, there is a possibility that at 100 degrees water freezes. It is an infinitesimal possibility (we can calculate it), but it exists.[28]

Information expresses the determination of probability, but it does not exclude beforehand the occurrence of the extremely unlikely. It is because communication, as a political technique, attempts to enclose an informational milieu around the informational couple 'actual/probable' that it also opens up another space – that of the fluctuations that produce the unpredictable, of the inventions that break the space of possibility, of the choices that are no choices at all but a kind of quantum jump onto another plane.

This is why the cultural politics of information can be said to bypass the relationship between the real and the possible to open up the relation between the real and the *virtual* – beyond the metaphysics of truth and appearance of the utopian imagination informing the revolutionary ideals of modernity. What lies beyond the possible, in fact, is not a utopian time and space to be realized against the harsh alienation of the present. This improbability that can only be predicted with the benefit of hindsight can be made to correspond to the category of the *virtual* – as it is formulated in the work of Henri Bergson, Gilles Deleuze and more recently Brian Massumi and

Pierre Levy.[29] The virtualization of a process involves opening up a real understood as devoid of transformative potential to the action of forces that exceed it from all sides. In an informational sense, the virtual appears as the site not only of the improbable, but of the openness of biophysical (but also socio-cultural) processes to the irruption of the unlikely and the inventive.

What lies beyond the possible and the real is thus the openness of the virtual, of the invention and the fluctuation, of what cannot be planned or even thought in advance, of what has no real permanence but only reverberations. Unlike the probable, the virtual can only irrupt and then recede, leaving only traces behind it, but traces that are virtually able to regenerate a reality gangrened by its reduction to a closed set of possibilities. Whether it is about the flash-like appearance and disappearance of the electronic commons (as in the early Internet), or the irruption in a given economic sector of a new technology able to unravel and disrupt its established organization of production (as in the current explosion of file-sharing systems), or whether it is about the virtuality of another world perceived during a mass demonstration or a workshop or a camp, the cultural politics of information involves a stab at the fabric of possibility, an undoing of the coincidence of the real with the given. In this sense, if we can talk about a cultural politics of information at all it is not because of new technologies, but because it is the reduction of the space of communication to a space of limited and hardly effectual alternatives (as in the postmodern sign) that poses the problem of the unlikely and the unthinkable as such. The cultural politics of information is no radical alternative that springs out of a negativity to confront a monolithic social technology of power. It is rather a *positive feedback effect* of informational cultures as such.

NONLINEARITY AND REPRESENTATION

From our previous discussion of entropy as a measure of uncertainty it seems reasonable to use the conditional entropy of the message, knowing the received signal, as a measure of this missing information.[30]

Proposition III: Information implies a nonlinear relation between the micro and the macro.

Corollary III: Within informational cultures, the centrality of the couple difference/position within a closed dialectics is displaced by that of mutation/movement within open systems.

Because information theory draws its theoretical underpinnings from thermodynamics and statistical mechanics, it understands material processes as implying a nonlinear relation between macrostates (such as averages, but also identities, subjectivities, societies and cultures) and microstates (the multiplicity of particles and interactions that underlie macrostates in as much as they also involve irreversible processes). This has a double consequence for our understanding of the cultural politics of information: on the one hand, it implies a shift away from representation to modulation which emphasizes the power of the mutating and divergent; on the other hand, it locates informational dynamics outside the perspectival and three-dimensional space of modernity and within an immersive, multidimensional and transformative topology.

For Jérôme Segal, we cannot really speak of a unified theory of information until the late 1940s, but we can definitely see how the preliminary labour started in fields such as statistics, physics and telecommunications at least since the 1920s. The question of information was posed first of all in the context of statistics of 'populations'. The question that the statistical theory of information addressed was that of

the scientific reduction of a mass of data to a relatively small number of quantities which must correctly represent this mass, or, in other words, must contain the largest possible part of the totality of relevant information contained in the original data.[31]

The mathematical tools through which this reduction was made possible were derived from the field of social physics as inaugurated in the mid nineteenth century by the Belgian astronomer Adolphe Quetelet (the inventor of the average man in society, a compiler of mortality and criminality tables and also the author of a statistical study on the 'propensity to suicide', which later came to provide the foundations of Emile Durkheim's famous sociological study). The modern theory of probability, however, had started as early as the mid seventeenth century, when a long-standing problem in games of dice was subjected to mathematical treatment.[32]

The statistical tools of probability theory had found a use in physics as well at least since James Clerk Maxwell started treating kinetic systems such as gases as 'collections of tiny particles rushing about at varying speeds and colliding with each other ... Since it is impossible to establish the exact speed of each particle, Maxwell treated the whole collection of particles statistically.'[33] At the end of the nineteenth century, Ludwig Boltzmann had established that since human beings could not know and should not be interested in the specific behaviour of each individual molecule at a particular moment, they could at least know how vast collections of particles behaved on average. As the system becomes more disorderly and temperature differences are lost, its entropy (the amount of 'energy unavailable for work') increases and even the limited knowledge allowed for by the average disappears: 'when the system is in a high state of entropy then it is *improbable* that [such parts] will be found in any special arrangement at a particular time'.[34] In a state of high entropy, both the randomness and the uncertainty with regard to the state of a system are at their maxima.

The entropy of a system thus corresponds to an uncertainty in our knowledge of it. Boltzmann's theorem identified a function H which measured the difference between the distribution of probabilities at any given time and those that exist at an equilibrium state of maximum entropy. As entropy increases and the system becomes more disorganized, the value of the function H would decrease and so would our knowledge of the probable state of any particle within the system. Shannon determined that Boltzmann's H-theorem also worked as a way to measure information.

Shannon repeatedly remarked how his theory of information was only concerned with the problem of communication engineering (and specifically the problem of the relation of noise to signal within a channel). And yet, the mathematical link that it established between information and entropy caused information theory to become the basis for the reunification of knowledge so much yearned for by twentieth-century science. The task of developing and expanding on the consequences of a quantitative definition of information fell to theorists such as Norbert Wiener (who published his bestselling book on cybernetics in the same year that Shannon's book was published and who, on the basis of seniority and prestige, claimed for himself priority over Shannon's work), Warren Weaver (director of the Rockefeller Foundation and author of a key explanatory essay on Shannon's theory) and later physicist Louis Brillouin, the controversial author of several texts on the relationship between information theory and science (such as *Science and Information*

Theory, in 1956; and *Scientific Uncertainty and Information,* in 1964). The first symposium on information theory took place in London in 1950, but it was the Macy conferences on cybernetics that really focused the scientific debate around information.

It is difficult to underestimate the resonance that the link between entropy and information had in the mid-twentieth-century scientific environment. Nineteenth-century thermodynamics identified through entropy a principle of irreversibility in physical processes, and more specifically a tendency of life to run out of differences and hence of available energy in its drive towards death. By identifying an equivalence between information and entropy, Shannon's work threw a bridge between the twentieth-century sciences of cybernetics and quantum theory and the nineteenth-century interest in heat engines, energy, irreversibility and death.

The link between information and entropy also referred back to a thinking experiment that had troubled physicists since the mid nineteenth century, Maxwell's Demon. The question posed by Maxwell's Demon was whether it was possible to counteract the tendency of closed systems to run out of energy, whether, that is, it was possible to identify a physical capacity that ran against the stream of entropy. The experiment suggested that a fictional being with perfect knowledge of the state of each individual molecule in a gas could counteract the increase of entropy within a heat engine by sorting out hot from cool molecules. The idea that Maxwell's Demon was nothing other than an abstract informational entity and that information involved an expenditure of energy had already been suggested – and with it the notion that information played a key role in the struggle of living organisms against the entropic tides that threatened them with death. As stated by quantum physicist Erwin Schrödinger in a key 1945 lecture, 'What is Life?', what needed to be explained for many physicists was not so much the physical tendency to dissipation that made all forms of life mortal, but its opposite. If the universe tended overall towards homogenization, life somehow expressed an upstream movement against the entropic tide. What is life if not negative entropy, a movement that runs against the second law of thermodynamics, whose existence is witnessed by the varieties of forms of life as they exist in the physical world? In asking a question that was to define the discourse of the life sciences for the next 50 years, Schrödinger argued that 'living organisms eat negative entropy' (that is, negentropy). Negentropic forces will thus be allocated a seat in the human organism – that of the macromolecule DNA, an informational microstructure able to produce living organisms by inducing the chemical reactions leading to the conversion of energy into differentiated types of cells.

This notion that information was somehow related to anti-entropic or negentropic forces is at the basis of the informationalist perspective that identifies information with a kind of form determining the material unfolding of life. Echoes of informationalism are present in all statements that argue that informational genetic sequences determine not only skin and hair colour, but even our very actions and feelings. This interpretation of the relation between information and entropy is not confirmed, however, by most of the current work in genetic or molecular biology, where the DNA macromolecule is understood as a simple inductor within the complex environment of the cell. Rather than expressing a deterministic relation between informational structures such as the DNA and a biophysical phenomenon such as the organism, the informational trend emphasizes the nonlinear relationship between molecular or micro levels of organization and molar or macro layers.[35] Like thermodynamics and statistical mechanics, information theory suggests that a macro-state or a molar formation (such as an average temperature; or an organism; or an 'identity') does not have a linear or deterministic relation to the multiplicity of the microscopic states that define it (the singular particles and their velocities; the microscopic relations that make up an organism; the mutations and variations that underlie all identities).

In its technical and scientific sense, then, information implies a 'representation' of a physical state, but there is no assumed resemblance between the representation and the state that it describes. Within the statistical model proposed by Quetelet's social physics, for example, the 'average' or 'norm' is the representation of a macrostate to which can correspond a variety of microstates. An average might be the same for a number of different possibilities (an average height of 6 feet in a population of 100 people might be realized by many different distributions of possible heights). As a macrostate, the average does not really exist, but it is a kind of social norm, a strange attractor endowed with the function to regulate the social body and stabilize it. It is the centre of gravity to which 'all the phenomena of equilibrium and its movement refers'.[36] Like the mass society that in those same years was increasingly preoccupying conservative and radical critics alike, thermodynamics and statistical mechanics too were concerned with formations such as masses, quantities such as averages and qualities such as homogeneity and heterogeneity. An average, however, can only adequately describe a low-entropy, highly structured system and its value as a descriptive measure is undermined in systems that are more fluid, hence more random and disorganized (such as the disorganized capitalism described by John Urry and Scott Lash, for example).[37] The state of a flow is always a function of the aggregate behaviour of a microscopical multiplicity, but as chaos theory showed, there is no linear and direct relation between the micro (the particles) and the macro (the overall flow dynamics). It is at the level of the micro, however, that mutations and divergences are engendered and it is therefore in the micro that the potential for change and even radical transformation lie.

This is why both cybernetics and the mathematical theory of communication involved a shift of representational strategies, such as a preference for the use of discrete quantities (such as digital code) over continuous ones. The difference is all in a relationship to microscopic levels of organizations that are understood as inherently metastable, characterized by sudden and discontinuous variations that the use of continuous quantities cannot capture with sufficient precision. Norbert Wiener, for example, discussed the problems with the continuous representation of physical states in terms of its intrinsic inadequacy in relation to the microscopic instability of the matter–energy continuum. For him, machines that represent the object by following and reproducing the variations in intensity of light, texture or sound on a material substrate always end up producing an unbridgeable gap between representation and reality, a gap which can only produce the dreaded interference of *noise*.

For cyberneticians the discrete cut implied by a digital code made up for the approximation inherent in continuous or analogous quantities (which can only capture a static average rather than the instability of the micro). In a passage that could be read in conjunction with Jean Baudrillard's theory of simulation, Wiener describes the problematic relation between a continuous representational technique (in this case a slide rule, but we could also say a map or an 'identity') and the object represented (the territory, or the actual individuals and pre-individual or unstable dimensions that they contain). For Wiener, analogue machines, unlike digital machines, *measure* rather than count, and are therefore 'greatly limited in their precision', because they operate 'on the basis of analogous connection between the measured quantities and the numerical quantities supposed to represent them'. Wiener points out how digital machines, on the other hand, offer 'great advantages for the most varied problems of communication and control...', in as much as 'the sharpness of the decision between "yes" and "no" permits them to accumulate information in such a way as to allow us to discriminate very small differences in very large numbers'.[38] If we compare a slide rule, for example, to a digital computer, we can clearly see how the accuracy of the former can only be approximate. The scale on which the marks have to be printed, the accuracy of our eyes, pose some very sharp limits to the precision with which the rule can be read. There is no point in trying to make the slide rule larger, because this increases the problems of accuracy.[39]

Any attempt at using continuous quantities to measure physical phenomena is thus doomed by a material impossibility: the nature of our perception (defined phenomenologically as the power of human eyes), which is imprecise; and the rigidity of analogue machines in general (which can only produce averages and identities whilst screening out all micro-variations and mutations as irrelevant exceptions, and hence miss change). These factors combine to make analogue techniques ultimately too limited. Even if the map could become as large as the territory, it would still be too rigid and inaccurate. Thus Wiener suggests that *numbers* are the best way to capture an intrinsically unstable and unmeasurable matter. Numbers in this case stand for a principle of discontinuity and microvariations which another famous cybernetician, Gregory Bateson, opposed to the continuity of quantities.

Between *two* and *three* there is a jump. In the case of quantity, there is no such jump and because the jump is missing in the world of quantity it is impossible for any quantity to be exact. You can have exactly three tomatoes. You can never have exactly three gallons of water. Always quantity is approximate.[40]

By extending the principle of counting to fractions and infinitesimal numbers, turning numbers into the infinite combinations of zeros and ones, digitization is able to produce exact and yet mobile snapshots of material processes. Such representations, however, are never either complete or exhaustive, because the relationship between the micro and the macro unfolds within a nonlinear mode. The result of this new closeness through numbers is a blurring: the closer you try to get to matter the faster your counting has to become in an attempt to catch up with the imperceptible speed of matter. Information theory accepts the existence of an 'incomplete determinism, almost an irrationality in the world ... a fundamental element of chance'.[41]

The crossover of information and communication techniques from scientific speculation to market research, from theoretical physics to cultural politics is too complex to map out here. What is relevant to the current discussion, however, is that the rise of the concept of information has contributed to the development of new techniques for collecting and storing information that have simultaneously attacked and reinforced the macroscopic moulds of identity (the gender, race, class, nationality and sexuality axes). Thus, the cultural politics of information does not address so much the threat of 'disembodiment', or the disappearance of the body, but its microdissection and modulation, as it is split and decomposed into segments of variable and adjustable sizes (race, gender, sexual preferences; but also income, demographics, cultural preferences and interests). It is at this point that we can notice the convergence of the cultural politics of information with digital techniques of decomposition and recombination. For Pierre Levy, 'digitisation is the absolute of montage, montage affecting the tiniest fragments of a message, an indefinite and constantly renewed receptivity to the combination, fusion and replenishment of signs'.[42] It is not only the messages that are fragmented and constantly renewed and recombined, but also the receivers of these messages, in the form of bits of information archived and cross-referenced through a million databases.

The emergence of information as a concept, then, should also be related to the development of a set of techniques, including marketing strategies and techniques of communication management – as they attempt to capture the increasing randomness and volatility of culture. Already in the early 1990s, the marketing literature was describing the shift from new media to the Internet in terms of information-targeting strategies. The New Economy apologists, for example, famously postulated three stages of media power: broadcasting, narrowcasting and pointcasting.[43] The latter corresponded to a digital mode in which messages were not simply directed at groups but tailored to individuals and even sub-individual units (or as Gilles Deleuze called them, 'dividuals', what results from the decomposition of individuals into data clouds subject to automated integration and disintegration). These patterns identified by marketing models correspond to a process whereby the postmodern segmentation of the mass audiences is pursued to the point where it becomes a mobile, multiple and discontinuous microsegmentation. It is not simply a matter of catering for the youth or for migrants or for wealthy entrepreneurs, but also that of disintegrating, so to speak, such youth/migrants/entrepreneurs into their microstatistical composition – aggregating and disaggregating them on the basis of ever-changing informational flows about their specific tastes and interests.

Information transmission and processing techniques, as exemplified in the technical machine that Lev Manovitch considers to be the arch-model of the new media, the database, have helped to discriminate and exploit the smallest differences in tastes, timetables and orientations, bypassing altogether the self-evident, humanistic subject, going from masses to populations of sub-individualized units of information. At the same time, this decomposition has not simply affected the identical, but also the different. Gender, race and sexuality, the mantra of the cultural politics of difference in the 1980s and 1990s, have been reduced to recombinable elements, disassociated from their subjects and recomposed on a plane of modulation – a close sampling of the micromutations of the social, moving to the rhythm of market expansions and contractions.

In this sense, the foregrounding of informational flows across the socius also implies a crisis of *representation* (both linguistic and political). The statistical modulation of information is highly disruptive in its relation to representation because it undermines the perspectival and three-dimensional space which functions as a support for relations of mirrors and reflections as they engender subjects, identities and selves.[44] In other words, the logic of representation presupposes a homogeneous space where different subjects can recognize each other when they are different and hence also when they are identical. This applies both at the level of linguistic representation (where I need to know what a man is in order to know what a woman is); but also at the level of political representation (as displayed in the allocation of positions across a political spectrum that is disposed from left to right as if facing an audience/public somehow always located at the centre). The analysis of the play of differences in representation within the self–other dialectics, in fact, has always implied the support of a space where the other is observed as from across a space. It is this empty space organized by a three-dimensional perspective that gives support to the psychic dynamics of identification, but also to the possibility of linguistic representation of the self and others as they are observed across such space. The space presupposed and engendered by an informational perspective expresses a radical challenge to representation – and hence also to the cultural politics of identity and difference. It is not only that all identities and even differences are reconfigured as macrostates or averages which belie a much more fluid and mutating composition. It is also that the whole configuration of space within which such politics were conceived has undergone a shift of focus.

The divergence between a representational and an informational space is illustrated by recent developments in robotics and artificial intelligence – two fields of research for which the relationship between representation and information is crucial. Rodney Brooks has given us some vivid descriptions of early efforts to build intelligent machines (such as mobile robots) able to navigate effectively through space. Most early efforts in mobile robotics (or *mobotics* as it is also known) relied on a *representational* approach to cognition and movement. A robot was provided with sensors (such as cameras) able to scan a space for obstacle and directions. The informational stream collected by the robot was translated into a two- or three-dimensional map that the robot would then use to navigate the environment. This approach was ultimately unsuccessful because the information contained in the environment ultimately exceeded the robot's computational capacity. The robot just could not make a map that was accurate enough – it often missed the relevant factors or picked the wrong ones.[45]

Brooks explains how the representational approach that assumed a relation between a three-dimensional space and a 'cognition box' able to provide a two- or three-dimensional map of reality which in its turn gave rise to an action ultimately failed. He sees this failure as an incapacity of such representation to keep up with the complexity and instability of an informational space (representation can only capture the macro-scale, but it misses the abundance of reality and its capacity for dynamic shifts). The robot was not immersing itself in the complexity of informational space, allowing its sensory organs to interact directly with the environment, but was, so to speak, keeping its distance from it in order to represent it. This distance was necessary to the completion of a three-dimensional map of the environment that it then used to navigate the space. (The visualization techniques used in this process laid the basis for developments in special effects and simulational training techniques). This operation was unbearably slow and it failed to deal even with a minimum alteration and the different levels of the environment. The mobotics approach, on the other hand, got rid of the cognition box, and instantiated a direct relationship between sensors and motors in ways that allowed the robot to interact directly with its environment (substituting the cognition box with a simple memory device). The loop between sensor and motor organs allowed a more direct and dynamic interaction with the huge informational flows generated even by the most simple environment. Space becomes informational not so much when it is computed by a machine, but when it presents an excess of sensory data, a radical indeterminacy in our knowledge, and a nonlinear temporality involving a multiplicity of mutating variables and different intersecting levels of observation and interaction. Space, that is, does not really need computers to be informational even as computers make us aware of the informational dimension as such. An informational space is inherently immersive, excessive and dynamic: one cannot simply observe it, but becomes almost unwittingly overpowered by it. It is not so much a three-dimensional, perspectival space where subjects carry out actions and relate to each other, but a field of displacements, mutations and movements that do not support the actions of a subject, but decompose it, recompose it and carry it along.

An engagement with the technical and scientific genealogy of a concept such as information, then, can be actively critical without disacknowledging its power to give expression and visibility to social and physical processes. We are very aware of the linguistic and social constraints that overdetermine the formation of scientific knowledge, and yet we cannot deny it a *dialogic* relationship with natural processes (as Ilya Prigogine and Isabelle Stengers have put it). As it informs and doubles into the social, the physical world that emerges out of this relationship is not passive, immutable, or even unknowable, but probabilistic, chaotic, indeterminate and open.

As I have described it, information is neither simply a physical domain nor a social construction, nor the content of a communication act, nor an immaterial entity set to take over the real, but a specific reorientation of forms of power *and* modes of resistance. On the one hand, it is about a resistance to informational forms of power as they involve techniques of manipulation and containment of the virtuality of the social; and on the other hand, it implies a collective engagement with the potential of such informational flows as they displace culture and help us to see it as the site of a *reinvention* of life. In every case, this reinvention today cannot really avoid the challenge of informational milieus and topologies. In as much as the network topos seems to match and embrace the turbulent involutions of such microcultural dynamics, the informational dimension of communication involves the emergence of *a network culture*. It is to the informational *topos* of the network, then, that we will keep turning to in order to catch this *active constitution* of informational cultures.

2
Network Dynamics

Machines, the reality constructed by capitalism, are not phantasms of modernity after which life can run unscathed – they are, on the contrary, the concrete forms according to which reality organizes itself, and the material connections within which subjectivity is produced. *Ordo et connexio rerum idem est ac ordo et connexio idearum.*[1]

NETWORK TIME

In 1998, taking its hint from McLuhan's notion of the global village, the Swatch corporation decided to introduce some standards into the chaotic tangle of Internet culture – a world where successive waves of global netsurfers would crowd chatrooms and online gaming sites, meeting and parting at the intersection of overlapping time zones, gathering as if they were passing down the torch of a sleepless, always up and on networked planet. If the Internet was unifying the globe through a common electronic space, then Swatch thought of itself as the most obvious candidate to provide the single time to match. In the corporate imagination, the new medium that had captured the time and attention span of a fickle and affluent global youth could be nothing else than an electronic metropolis, in dire need of some kind of time standard. The Swiss corporation thus launched a new global or Internet time, divided into 'swatch beats', each beat corresponding to a little more than one minute. Thus if 'a New York based web-surfer makes a date for a chat with a cyber-friend in Rome, they can simply agree to meet at an "@ time", because Internet time is the same all over the world'.[2] The Swatch time was a sleek attempt to link the transcendental globalization of the planet achieved by the 1990s global consumer culture to a new type of globalization – grafting the power of the brand on that of the internetwork.

As Geert Lovink recounts, Swatch's Internet time was just one of at least three attempts to propose a 'spaceless, virtual time standard, located within networks no longer referring to Greenwich mean time'.[3] For Lovink, these attempts demonstrated how '[t]he legacy of our inherited 19th-century temporal model segmenting the planet into 24 separate time zones (and two simultaneous dates) increasingly no longer fits well with our nascent third-millennium global temporal perceptions'.[4] This idea of a global time corresponding to the global space of the Internet goes to the heart of the problem posed by the Internet and its relation to the world of locality – where the local is often made to coincide with the real, the heterogeneous and the embodied. This debate has recently come to overlap with an earlier perspective that considered computer networks mainly as expressions of dematerialization and disembodiment. The everyday use of the Internet, its implication in the ordinary work of learning, working, and communicating, has done much to dismantle the notion of cyberspace as virtual reality. On the other hand, it is undeniable that the Internet has joined media such as television and cinema as one of the great accused in the trial about the *virtual globalization* (and related technocultural imperialism) of the planet.[5]

As geographers have pointed out, one of the most fundamental aspects of communication lies in the ways in which it forms and deforms the fabric of space and time. Communication technologies do more than just link different localities. Pathways and roads, canals and railways, telegraphs and satellites modify the speed at which goods, ideas, micro-organisms, animals and people encounter and transform each other. They actively mould what they connect by creating new topological configurations and thus effectively contributing to the constitution of geopolitical entities such as cities and regions, or nations and empires. The rise of the nation and nationalism in the nineteenth century, for example, would have been unthinkable without the centralized pull of the railway system, the homogenizing embrace of national newspapers and the synchronizing power of national broadcasting corporations. Of late, the layered communication system modelled on the nation state has witnessed another mutation with the rise of global, real-time communication networks such as satellite television and computer networks. As should be expected, such reconfiguration of the overall communication system is linked to the emergence of new geopolitical formations and in particular it seems inextricably linked to the open and unbounded space of the post-cold-war global empire, as described in Michael Hardt and Antonio Negri's homonymous book.[6]

The communication topology of Empire is complex as it is woven together by aeroplanes, freight ships, television, cinema, computers and telephony, but what all these different systems seem to have in common is their convergence on the figure not simply of the network, but a kind of *hypernetwork, a meshwork potentially connecting every point to every other point.* As such, the network is becoming less and less a description of a specific system, and more a catchword to describe the formation of a single and yet multidimensional information milieu – linked by the dynamics of information propagation and segmented by diverse modes and channels of circulation.

If the network topos does not and cannot be made to coincide with the Internet, the latter however expresses an interesting mutation of the network diagram in its relation to the cultural and political assemblages of this twenty-first century neo-imperial formation. A brainchild of a US Defense research programme and, for a while, the spearhead of another US-led economic revolution, a global medium with a fast rate of diffusion in Third World countries, a global means of organization, the medium of the multitude, a market for technological innovations, a soapbox for opinionated individuals, a means of collective organization, a challenge to the regime of intellectual property, a new publishing platform, electronic agora, cyber-bazaar, sleaze factory and global junkyard – some would argue that the Internet can only be described in a piecemeal, empirical fashion and in any case as an 'unrepresentative' medium in its relation to wider processes of globalization.

It is true that in terms of the actual power to capture the passions of the global masses, the Internet is no match for the reach and power of television, which, from local and national broadcasting channels to satellite TV such as CNN and Al-Jazeera, can count on the wider accessibility of the necessary technology (the TV set) and on the high impact of images and sounds broadcast in real time. Neither can we deny the minority status of Internet users on a global scale, considering that no medium can transcend the economic chasm widened by the neoliberal policies of the 'Washington Consensus' in the 1980s and 1990s.[7] If the Internet appears to us as such a key global communication technology, it is not because of overwhelming numbers or mass appeal (although it is true that it has witnessed an explosive global growth in just over a decade). It is rather because, unlike the other global communication technologies mentioned above, it has been conceived and evolved as a *network of networks*, or an internetwork, a topological formation that presents some challenging insights into the dynamics underlying the formation of a global network culture. As a technical system, the Internet consists of a set of interrelated protocols, abstract technical diagrams that give the network consistency beyond the rapidly changing hardware environment of computers, servers, cable and wires. Even though basic Internet protocols have changed over time, the philosophy that has informed their design and hence the architecture of the Internet has been consistent overall and informed by a few key principles which have, up until this moment, survived scalability (such as a universal address space, a layered and modular structure, the distributed movements of data packets and the interoperability of heterogeneous systems). Such principles imply a strong conception of an informational milieu as a dynamic topological formation, characterized by a tendency towards divergence and differentiation, posing the problem of *compatibility* and the production of a *common space* as an active effort involving an unstable or metastable milieu. In other words, beyond being a concrete assemblage of hardware and software, the internetwork is also an abstract technical diagram implying a very specific production of space. As we will see, what characterizes the technical diagram and design principles that have driven the development of the Internet is a tendency to understand space in terms of the biophysical properties of *open systems*. By modelling such open network spatiality the Internet becomes for us more than simply one medium among many, but a kind of general figure for the processes driving the globalization of culture and communication at large.

OF GRIDS AND NETWORKS

The relation between the Internet and the production of space is, by no chance, crucial to all theoretical and analytical engagement with Internet culture. A feature of this engagement has been its insistence on such informational space as being somehow characterized by a dangerous distance from the world of the flesh and of physical spaces. If the early debate on information networks was dominated by the image of a Gibsonian cyberspace in which users would lose consciousness of the real world and lose themselves in a universe of abstract forms and disembodied perspectives, the contemporary debate has shifted onto the terrain of globalization. Where the most common image of cyberspace used to be that of a virtual-reality environment characterized by direct interface and full immersion (data gloves, goggles, embedded microchips and electrodes), now the image is that of a common space of information flows in which the political and cultural stakes of globalization are played out. The debate on a transcendental cyberspace in opposition to the world of the flesh has developed its counterpart in a political discourse that opposed the homogeneous pull of the global to the heterogeneous world of locality.

For geographers such as Manuel Castells, for example, the network makes explicit the dynamics by which a globally connected elite is coming to dominate and control the lives of those who remain bound to the world of locality, thus reinforcing a 'structural domination of the space of flows over the space of places'.[8] According to this perspective, in network societies the concrete time of places, bound to a specific mode of duration, is increasingly subsumed by the *imperium* of a single, electronic and global space accessible at the click of a mouse: 'the edge of forever or timeless time'. Paul Virilio has argued for the opposite and specular case: information networks are annihilating space in favour of time (thus the Gulf Wars were global, not because they happened in a global space as did World War II, but because they happened in global time, the single time or 'real time' of global television and the Internet). If world history is marked by a constant acceleration (from the age of horses and carriages to that of bullet trains and intercontinental missiles), the emergence of global information networks marks a limit point, as if with global communication we had hit a wall and started a detonation. Thus the simultaneity of actions has taken precedence over the succession of events and the world has been reduced to one unique time and space – 'an accident without precedent'.[9] The time of the network is 'real time': everything happens simultaneously and thus fatalistically with a kind of after-the-event sense of inevitability.

When we relate such allegations to the abstract technical diagrams that make an electronic space such as the Internet possible, we find that they seem to correspond to a specific aspect of its information architecture. To be locatable on the Internet, in fact, a machine/host/user needs to have an address and this address needs to be unequiv-ocally situated within a common address space. This ecumenical function (the function of creating a single space) is performed by the Internet Protocol (IP) and the Domain Name System (DNS). This Internet Protocol has undergone a number of changes over the years but its main function has not really changed: it is the code that assigns to each machine an individual number. The Domain Name System associates each number with a cell in a table and also gives it a name. The DNS is thus an ideal single spatial map of the Internet, comprising a system of unique addresses that makes each IP-coded host and server locatable. Whenever we type an email address or a URL into the apposite program, we are to all effects referring to a specific address in this global, electronic map. This feature of the Internet design confirms the image of a distance between a world of information and a world of embodied and bounded locality.

Furthermore, this informational and electronic space, as it is constituted within this single map, appears as uncannily reminiscent of a modern dream for a completely homogeneous and controllable space. If we compare the Internet to a global city, with its addresses and neighbourhoods, its overall layout as expressed by the DNS database structure is hypermodernist. Its global electronic address space is structured like a grid of discrete locations – all of which from the point of view of the system have an equal probability of being accessed. In informational terms, that is, the Internet is in principle a highly entropic system (hence tendentially homogeneous) in as much as it can be entered at any point and each movement is in principle as likely as the next. In principle, that is, each Internet browser or file transfer protocol or email programme is structurally free to jump to any street and house number whatsoever (to continue our urban analogy). In order to limit the demands posed on the technical system by such high entropic levels of randomness and indetermination, the DNS protocol divides such single space through a limited number of top-level domains (.com, .org, .net, .edu, and the national domains, such as .uk, .au, etc) enclosing it, so to speak, at the top.[10] Each domain is infinitely divisible: it is divided into a series of subdomains and each subdomain in its turn is potentially composed of an infinite number of smaller addresses, neatly branching out from its umbrella to identify individual users or machines, from servers to personal computers to all kinds of communication devices. (There is a movement to extend the IP protocol to Internet-connectable electric appliances and objects such as toasters, fridges and clothes.)

At the same time, however, this abstract and homogeneous space of cells and grids is not completely devoid of any physical relation to locality. To this abstract space able to contain all possible addresses corresponds a concrete assemblage of technical machines, the DNS servers, which are arranged in a hierarchical structure. Thirteen root servers, ten of which are currently located in the USA, two in Europe and one in Asia, for example, contain information about the next set of DNS machines, that is the authoritative name servers. There are as many authoritative name servers as there are domains and each one of them contains information about all the machines in that domain; the same is true for subdomains and so on. Thus, if the abstract Internet space is a grid in principle equally accessible from all points, in practice the speed and even, as we shall see, the trajectory by which we can actually get from A to B is determined by the relation and state of traffic between the servers, a relation that crucially includes the differential speeds of bandwidth and the 'weighting' of connections (where some nodes or cell-space assume centrality when compared to others). Finally, to the relatively centralized structure of the naming system corresponds a centralized governing body – a kind of global regulatory board. While the DNS was famously run for years and single-handedly by Internet pioneer Jon Postel, since his death it has been supervized by a non-profit organization, ICANN (Internet Corporation for Assigned Names and Numbers) – a corporation that has typically been the subject of heated controversies about accountability and democratic governance of the Internet.[11]

Another way in which the abstract space of the grid is modified and differentiated is through its relation to the semantic domain of the name (and specifically the semiotic economy of the brand name). The identification of IP addresses with names has introduced into Internet space the symbolic capital of brands – and hence has determined another differentiation at the heart of the universal information space, that of electronic real estate. Following the opening up of the Internet to commercial organizations, for example, the struggles around domain names have witnessed some spectacular lawsuits as corporations, speculators and activists looking for a fight rushed to get their hands on valuable names and addresses.[12] Within the gridded space of the DNS, the brand re-emerges as a star, a centre of gravity, an identifiable name that guides the netsurfer through the anonymous space of the IP number world. The tangled and heterogeneous meshwork that constitutes the Internet is thus not simply reconciled within the hieratic indifference of a universal information space, but also subjected to heated and controversial political debates, expensive litigations and cultural struggles. The Domain Name System then is both single and universal, but also formed and deformed by locality. For Tim Berners-Lee, the legal disputes around names correspond to a *friction* between electronic space and local space, which is where the DNS, overall, can be said to exist.

Trademark law assigns corporate names and trademarks within the scope of the physical location of businesses and the markets in which they sell. The trademark-law criterion of separation in location and market does not work for domain names, because the Internet crosses all geographic bounds and has no concept of market area, let alone one that matches the existing conventions in trademark laws.[13]

And yet, beyond the distortions introduced in the realm of Internet domains by the injection of symbolic capital, we cannot deny that at least in principle the Internet is organized through the figure of the grid and that this grid constitutes one of the most privileged references in theoretical understanding of electronic space. The grid is a fascinating figure and one with a particularly strong resonance within social and cultural theory, because of its strong association with the space of reason and modernity. The modernist grid, as defined by the intersection of two Cartesian axes, is a triumph of a mind able to extract a homogeneous and ordered space out of the ruggedness and heterogeneity of topological space. There is always something both utopian and dystopian about a grid. Whether it is a city plan, a prison layout or an accountant's spreadsheet, the grid is a principle of division and order, making possible the counting and location of things. If the Internet is ultimately reducible to a modernist form such as the grid, then the main movement that traverses it and organizes it is the vectorial movement of a tele-command.[14] An electronic address does not simply indicate a location within cyberspace (I am @ *anyplace*) but also the possible movement of a direct line traced between two points. (You can find me @ *anytime*. This document is at www.*anyplace*.org; you can find it there *whenever*). Information is divided and allocated a space, each node is assigned a unique number/name, and all information is instantly retrievable by way of a simple command line. Information is uploaded and downloaded as in a kind of electronic warehouse where new content is deposited and disposed of, deleted, updated, or simply left there to rot.

The connection between different locales on the grid is activated by the tele-command – by the click of a link activating the server's call for a response by the corresponding machine. It is in this sense, as some have remarked, that the Internet might not be an immersive virtual reality as the cyberpunks imagined it, but an alternative space existing 'at the edge of forever', as Manuel Castells put it. Cyberspace exists in the omni-equal distance that lies at the end of a mouse click. Regardless of the semantic differentiation of the IP address system, regardless of the geopolitical distribution of servers, within such a common informational plane a site in South Korea is ultimately within the same vectorial reach as a page in Rio. The whole planet feels as if it were compressed into the same virtual space just the other side of a computer screen, but it is as if such space was ultimately a static one, absorbing and neutralizing all differences on a single plane of communication.

Within this understanding, the Internet is thus nothing more than an extended database, crossed by repeatable sequences of commands enabling the retrieval of documents located at different points in the planet. This chilling picture of a single information space, divided and distributed on a single grid containing all the possible addresses of all possible machines, underlines many of the more damning descriptions of the Internet and its relationship to the world of locality and embodiment. From this perspective, the single information space is an extension of a modern instrumental rationality driving towards the ultimate goal of the disappearance of the irreducible heterogeneous in the homogeneous space of the global network. The Internet thus appears to give form to a space of connections without transformations, where vectors of communication link up different electronic spaces outside of any real possibility for becoming. But does the database structure really exhaust all aspects of network communication? Or does an over-reliance on the database model blind us to the more dynamic aspects of the Internet diagram and its relation to network culture as such?

THE PARADOX OF MOVEMENT

The debate about space and time in the age of communication is not necessarily limited to the Internet as such but is a variation on the larger theme of cultural globalization. A communication technology such as the Internet participates in the emergence of a globalized culture, following and expressing the fractal folds of a spatiality that twists and knots together different scales of interaction – the local and the global, but also the regional and the national. In as much as the Internet is an informational diagram, form here should not be understood in the sense of a mould, imprinting its stamp on a world of locality already weakened by decades of global popular culture. The Internet informs a globalized planet by reproducing some of its most individuated and stable forms as well as its potential to diverge, to pass over into new formations through the combined power of the fluctuation and the mutation.

Physicists such as Duncan J. Watts and Albert László Barabási, for example, have mapped 'the small worlds' of networks in terms of a relation between 'structure' and 'dynamics'.[15] Within the same field, Steve Lawrence and Lee Giles at the NEC Research Institute in Princeton have produced a model of the Web, based on the data brought back by a meta-search engine or robot about its size and topology. In this way, they have reconstructed the virtual geography of the World Wide Web by mapping the number of links that connect different web sites to each other. Replicating an action that search engines carry out all the time, algorithms have been let loose on the network to come back with a picture not only of how many pages and sites are actually out there on the Web, but also of the overall movement of information flows within the network. This approach downplays the links to locality (mapping the global distribution of Internet access) for an internal snapshot of the web world. The researchers thus looked not only for the number of pages and their location in the DNS grid (as a search engine bot would do), but also for the overall map drawn by the active movement of the link.

The result is a kind of parallel global map of an informational planet, produced on the basis of outgoing and incoming links, mapping the directed movement linking sites to sites. One such map pictured the informational space of the web-planet through the topology of continents, archipelagos and islands.[16] It mapped the gravitational pulls of portals and brands (at the heart of the core continents lie all the major websites – the likes of Yahoo, MSN, Google, the CNN and BBC – which collected the largest number of incoming links) and also the existence of peripheral information land masses, tied to a central core, but also independent from it. Beyond these massive continents signalling a centralization of Internet traffic, they pictured a sprinkling of small archipelagos made up of web sites that connect only to each other, and large info-islands which corresponded to Gibson's Black Ice – the firewalls hiding the high-security intranetworks of military and financial institutions. At the same time, the researchers admit that it was hard to claim that their map of web space is exhaustive – in as much as a great number of web sites appear to be off the radar. If the portals act as centripetal forces of attraction in an unstable and disorienting network space, producing the effect of an informational land mass, this does not exclude the existence of other movements of divergence and disconnection, which characterize, for example, the choice of some groups to communicate only with each other within a closed network of sites shielded from outside access by obscure addresses or corporate firewalls. In this sense, the global appears as a site of *accumulation* of resources that manifests itself as a *mass*, which distorts the homogeneous informational milieu by exercising a kind of gravitational pull that *draws in* other spatial scales (such as national or regional) to itself. Any interface with the medium, therefore, implies some kind of relation to such centripetal movement.

On the other hand, however, this centripetal and homogenizing pull of the global mass is not the only movement active within the Internet as an informational milieu. In this sense, we can draw a useful parallel with the debate on globalization. If a structural domination of the space of flows (the global) over that of places (the local) exists, together with attendant forms of cultural imperialism, it is one that does not deny the *fluidity of places as such*, their constitution as local reservoirs endowed with a productive capacity for difference. The study of global popular culture in the 1990s has gone some way towards mapping some of the features of this 'virtual global'. When seen spatially, a global culture has often appeared as split between the opposing pulls of homogenizing (global) and heterogenizing (local) forces. The relationship between the opposing poles of the global and the local has been shown to produce all kinds of mutant cultural forms – ranging from familiar patterns of pseudo-individuation (the French McDonald's as distinct from the American McDonald's, as depicted in the memorable dialogue between John Travolta and Samuel Jackson in *Pulp Fiction*), to more complex nonlinear dynamics of mutual feedback (as in the relationship between the cinemas of Hong Kong and Hollywood).[17]

If the local, in fact, were nothing but a reservoir of frozen differences; if the global were only the homogenizing pull of the likes of McDonald's, Microsoft and Coca-Cola; if the Internet were nothing but an electronic grid or database where all locations lie flat and movement is mainly that of vectors of fixed length but variable position linking distant locations to a few centres – where would the potential for struggle and change, becoming and transformation come from? In the case of the Internet, for example, where would its dynamism come from? How can we reconcile the grid-like structure of electronic space with the *dynamic* features of the Internet, with the *movements* of information? How do we explain chain mails and list serves, web logs and web rings, peer-to-peer networks and denial-of-service attacks? What about the rising clutter of information, the scams and the spam, the endless petitions, the instantaneous diffusion of noise and gossip, the network as permanent instability? It is possible, that is, that by thinking of the Internet in terms of the grid we might have fallen into a classic metaphysical trap: that of reducing duration to movement, that is, of confusing time with space.[18]

The notion that cyberspace is nothing more than the intersection of the grid and the vector reminds us of some classic paradoxes of movement – paradoxes that Henri Bergson referred to repeatedly in his dissection of Western metaphysics' relation to duration. The Zeno paradox, for example, marked a high point of confrontation between the pre-Socratic philosophy of qualitative change and the Euclidean geometry of position. The challenge of the former to the latter was thrown on the basis of the geometrical argument that between a point A and a point B lie an infinite number of points ($A...$ $B... C... D...$). Zeno's paradox was that of applying the geometrical method to motion: If an arrow has to pass through an infinity of points, how will it ever reach its target? How could Achilles catch up with a tortoise if in order to do so he will have to go through an infinity of points (which, in Euclidean geometry, compose a line)? Won't he be caught up in the infinite passage from point A to point B to point C and so on? Bergson's reading of Zeno's paradoxes is that they showed how the specificity of duration is unaccountable on the basis of the notion of an infinitely divisible space, a notion that deprives space of its qualitative dimension. Movement does not so much imply a simple passage between points, but involves duration, that is a qualitative becoming that affects both the arrow, the target, the archer and the overall context. Space is subdivided into discrete points only because the pragmatic orientation of our bodies in the world privileges space as a homogeneous container of objects and underestimates the fact that extension and duration are related within the process of becoming.

Bergson suggested that Western metaphysics (and hence also the popular metaphysics that gives rise to what we think of as 'common sense') is particularly troubled by the notion of an *intensive space,* a space that endures. Indeed Western metaphysics for Bergson has persistently misunderstood duration, almost as if it constituted a kind of unthinkable other. When we think about movement, Bergson argued, we make the common mistake of thinking of it as always the movement of an object through a space. We tend to think of something that moves as something that crosses a space that can be neatly assigned a position between a point of departure (A) and a point of arrival (*B*) through a whole series of intermediate points in between. Such a conception of movement divides it, that is, into two abstract formations: on the one side a homogeneous time (the time that is, that says that a plane leaves at 17:00 and arrives at 21:00); on the other side a homogeneous space (the space in which the plane can always be located at a definite longitude and latitude). The notion that the Internet annihilates the heterogeneity of times onto a single space can only make sense within such a metaphysical understanding of the space–time relation. If a command, such as that which calls up a web page in India or California, employs more or less the same time to reach any-destination-whatsoever, then there is no time at all. Only a single, hypercontracted, supergrid of a space. Bergson explained this understanding of movement in terms of a line linking two positions with the necessary illusion by which our perception screens out the blurred complexity of duration in order to isolate definite objects that can be manipulated. Necessary as this reduction sometimes is, for Bergson it cannot produce a proper understanding of becoming. What is time, then, if it is not the seconds or hours or days that it takes to go from *A* to *B*? What is movement within electronic space if it is not the linear command of a client–server exchange, the instant flashing of a message, the click on a link, the immediate openness of everybody and everything to everybody and everything else?

For Bergson, by thinking of movement as a linear translation of an object through space we miss a fundamental element: the *virtuality* of duration, the qualitative change that every movement brings not only to that which moves, but also to the space that it moves in and to the whole into which that space necessarily opens up. A plane journey, for example, is not simply about bringing a big, metal, flying machine with a bunch of passengers from *A* to *B*. The plane's movement affects the space it moves in and modifies it. It transforms the chemical composition of the atmosphere. It affects the passengers and staff through a transformation or qualitative change in their relationship with what they have left while they wait to change what they are moving towards. A piece of information spreading throughout the open space of the network is not only a vector in search of a target, it is also a potential transformation of the space crossed that always leaves something behind – a new idea, a new affect (even an annoyance), a modification of the overall topology. Information is not simply transmitted from point *A* to point *B*: it propagates and by propagation it affects and modifies its milieu.

While Western metaphysics looks at movement as a function of a homogeneous, hence unchangeable space and time, Bergson suggests that we should understand movement always in relation to the open whole, that is the whole duration that it affects. Duration implies a qualitative transformation of space and space itself is nothing but an ongoing movement opening onto an unbounded whole.

> Thus in a sense movement has two aspects. On the one hand that which happens between objects or parts; on the other hand that which expresses the duration or the whole... We can therefore say that movement relates the objects of a closed system to open duration, and duration to the objects of the system, which it forces to open up.[19]

Although grounded in some aspects of its own technical structure, the notion that the Internet is just a new stage in the constitution of a global culture where distance and locality are annihilated does not do justice to such informational dynamics. At a practical level, for example, we might point out that the space of the grid is much more mobile and dynamic than it appears – with individual users using more than one machine, or disappearing and reappearing from the network at different times using different aliases or identities. At the same time the linkages established by the tele-command of electronic space, by the call-and-response mode of the distributed database, do not lead to a single time or space, but to a multiple duration where linkages constitute a fluid dynamic of connection and differentiation. However, even a partial modification of our description of the grid–vector model, does not do justice to the dynamic capacity of network culture to renew and modify the medium – not simply by moving information around, but by deforming and differentiating the overall network milieu. If the Internet is a form linking the bounded with the unbounded, the local with the global, then it is a particularly dynamic one. To take the duration of the network seriously demands that our analysis should relate its most stratified and organized moments (the grid space of the DNS; the vectors of tele-command; the stellar power of the brand system) to other aspects of internetworking (packet switching; open architecture; network culture). It is not by chance that we find this conception of space as duration within two of the other most basic and emblematic Internet design principles: open architecture and packet switching.

A TENDENCY TO DIFFER

> ... all *innovative, creative* systems are *divergent*, conversely, sequences
> of events that are predictable are, ipso facto, convergent.[20]

If we managed the impossible task of freeze-framing the Internet for a second, we would be faced with a bewildering picture. Starting with the most popular Internet activity, emailing, we would undoubtedly be struck by the sheer magnitude of a traffic that eludes all measurement (estimates point to billions of messages exchanged per day).[21] A change of perspective would reveal how this popular Internet protocol entails a small galaxy of different modes – ranging from the exchanges of individual emails to the pack movement of spam to the mobilizing command of office mailing lists to the open spirals scattered throughout by discussion groups. Besides the movement of email packets, we would also undoubtedly be struck by the vast expanse of the World Wide Web, a veritable info-planet that computer models have reconstructed as entailing its own geography of a densely populated land mass (the portal phenomenon), surrounded by smaller continents, and little archipelagos of disconnected islands.[22] A close-up of the fringes would reveal staggering clusters of file-sharing, peer-to-peer networks and parallel computing. If we zoomed in to look at the details we would be able to see the electronic bulletin board systems and the social software zones – from dating agencies to community web logs and wikis. Finally, if we looked hard enough, we would probably be able to see the open-source and free software programming sites, spinning the web from within their relatively small but highly effective network enclaves. This synchronic slice of internetworking would highlight the layered and overlapping topologies of the single communication space. However it is with *time*, that is in its dynamic dimensions, that this topology reveals a larger picture of merging micro-waves of technological innovation that over relatively short spans of time have considerably enriched the social experience of electronic communication (from telnet, ftp, email, irc, muds to http, streaming, blogs, p2p, wi-fi, wikis, etc.).

What makes the Internet a challenging medium is not only the nature of its technological components but more generally the design principles that have informed its ongoing evolution. The Internet, in fact, is not just a global computer network, but a network of networks, the actualization of a set of design principles entailing the interoperability of heterogeneous information systems. Not only, that is, is there no central control of the Internet (although there are many control centres), but the whole space of communication has been designed and conceived in terms of dynamic and variable relations between different communication networks.[23] The Internet was conceived from its inception as a heterogeneous network, able to accommodate in principle, if not in actuality, not only diverse communication systems, but also drifting and differentiating communication modes.

If we look at the architecture of the Internet as a turning-point within the history of communication, in fact, this turning-point does not simply coincide with the set-up of the first ARPANET connection in 1969 – traditionally held to be the birth of the Internet. The first dedicated computer network to span a number of institutions across the USA, ARPANET was certainly an important technological breakthrough, but it was still not the Internet. ARPANET carried through the consequences of a conceptual revolution in computing that shifted the emphasis from computers as calculating machines to computers as communication devices – at first by way of time sharing and subsequently through local and wide area networks.

Around the time when the first computer network was devised, the whole approach to computing was undergoing a singular revolution. The old notion of a computer as a task-oriented, mechanical device to which white-coated lab scientists would respectfully take their more complex calculations was giving way to a focus on interactivity within a cybernetic and informational perspective on communication. Among those scientists who were involved with research at DARPA, for example, we find J. C. R. Licklider, who advocated the notion of a 'man–computer' symbiosis that could both speed up some of the more routine aspects of scientific work and free up a new capacity for conceptual innovation. Others, like Douglas Engelbart, pioneered devices such as the mouse, time sharing and the visual display of information, intended to facilitate the collectivity of technical thinking. The ARPANET team tested and introduced packet switching – a technical innovation that allowed the maximum exploitation of bandwidth for the purposes of data communication; designed the system by thinking of network users as potential contributors to the system's development, thus paving the way for the endlessly mutating future Internet; publicized the results of the experiment outside the DARPA network in computer conferences and public journals; and trained PhD students who were later to make an essential contribution to the emergence of business and grassroots networks.

In spite of the fact that ARPANET was the first computer network, however, it did not really include some of the key principles of network architecture that characterize the Internet today. Some people claim that the real 'birthday' of the Internet was four years later, that is 1 January 1973. This change is identified with the switch-over from NCP to TCP/IP, that is, from a closed network model that drew clear boundaries around the network and maintained a measure of centralized control to an open architecture model that was designed as intrinsically open to new additions. As an article on the net-magazine *Telepolis* argued

[t]he change from one big packet switching network under the control of one administrative or political structure to an open architecture allowing for communication among dissimilar networks under diverse forms of political or administrative structures, is the change that has made it possible to have an international Internet today.[24]

Open architecture was part of a more general effort by computer scientists to think anew the question of the organization of networks and electronic space. Introduced by Robert Kahn and Vincent Cerf at DARPA, open architecture networking assumes that individual networks may be separately designed and developed, using their own specific and unique interfaces to fit the user requirements and the environment in which they operate. Whatever the interface or scope of individual networks, whether small, local area networks or intercontinental, wide area ones, the design philosophy of open architecture dictates that they should all be equally allowed to connect to the internetwork and hence to each other by way of a system of gateways and routers directing traffic between them on a best-effort basis. This process involves the design of common protocols that are meant to impose no internal change on the participating networks. Each network is thus assumed to be autonomous, that is, able to stand on its own even outside its Internet connection (thus if the Internet were to break down, individual networks would simply lose their connections to each other but internal use should still be possible). No internal changes or global control are thus required (except, as we have seen, for some coordination at the DNS level and open technical boards in charge of maintaining consistency of standards).

The individual networks might even decide to keep part of their operations closed or to filter out most outside traffic.[25] The decision of individual networks to close the flow of information however would not affect the overall topology that tends towards the production of a smooth, open and unbounded space.

The development of open architecture within computing stands in marked contrast to parallel developments in architecture of the bricks-and-mortar variety. While in the late 1970s urban architecture went through the postmodern moment of Venturi's *Learning From Las Vegas*, the still marginal field of information architecture introduced an alternative conception of spatial organization. If architects were moving away from the purist excesses of high modernism towards the heterogeneous pastiches of postmodernity, information architects and engineers were working out the blueprints of a similar and yet alternative problematic of space. Within open architecture, in fact, electronic space is not conceived as composed of different fragments, juxtaposed together in a *pastiche* mode, as in postmodern architecture. The different components accommodated by open architecture are not inert fragments of living or dead styles, but autonomous networks in continuous expansion and modification. Open architecture provided the field of computer networks with a common framework based on a pragmatic grasp of the inevitability of spatio-temporal differentiation.[26] As an RFC (Request for Comments) document of the Network Working Group put it, 'The [Internet's] architectural principles ... aim to provide a framework for creating cooperation and standards, as a small "spanning set" of rules that generates a large, varied and evolving space of technology.'[27]

In as much as there is no limit to the number of networks that open architecture can accommodate, the development of internetworking technologies is crucially concerned with modulating the relationship between differentiation and universality. As Paul Baran demonstrated in his 1960s research on packet switching, centralized networks are extremely vulnerable both to technical failures and to targeted enemy attacks. Command functions need to be distributed, thus allowing a communication network to survive the destruction of a high percentage of its nodes. At the same time, such distribution of command functions once applied to a system that is conceived as always potentially open to new additions carries within itself a tendency to divergence and differentiation that in the absence of a coherent design strategy can easily lead to catastrophic transformations (such as the breakdown of the network in secluded territories). Removed from the central controlling gaze of a single centre, space tends not so much to fragment into individual cells, as to diverge, hybridizing itself around the peculiar features of different milieus and cultures. Decentralized and distributed networks, although intrinsically more robust and resilient than centralized ones, present the intrinsic problem of a tendency towards differentiation and drift that threatens to turn the open network into an archipelago of disconnected and isolated islands.

This tendency of decentralized networks to diverge to the point of disconnection is described by open architecture as a tendency towards the production of *incompatibilities*. Divergence brings with it the tendency towards disconnection and disconnection produces incompatibilities. The adaptability and flexibility inherent in the shift away from expensive mainframes towards microcomputers and eventually personal computers makes computer networks particularly liable to modifications and mutations, to specialized uses inherent in the multiplicity of contexts into which computing spreads.

The networking of computers, the emergence of different networking cultures in the 1970s and 1980s, only confirmed the intuition of open architecture: resilience needs decentralization; decentralization brings localization and autonomy; localization and autonomy produce differentiation and divergence. Within open architecture, such divergent movements are not supposed to disappear once and for all once the initial incompatibilities are overcome. Incompatibilities set up by the drift of divergent movements are the limits that open networks continuously generate and must also overcome. An open network should always be potentially extensible, and therefore should be structurally equipped to deal with irreconcilable tensions by leaping to a new level of generality that would thus allow such differences to connect within a common space. This level of generality must involve a structural openness able to accommodate the *duration* of the network at large.

A brief technical history of the development of internetworking, from ARPANET to the World Wide Web, clearly shows the recurrence of the problem of divergence and incompatibility. The ARPANET researchers, for example, have often insisted that the military needs for a resilient communication network were not the direct motivation behind the development of computer networks. Resilience was important, of course: the Internet *was* built to be robust. But, they say, this was *not* the main drive behind the development of internetworking technologies, not even behind the controversial adoption of packet switching. The main problem, they explain, was not a nuclear attack, but the tendency towards the production of *incompatibilities*:

> The core problem of getting computers to communicate with each other is, by definition, one of compatibility. As the network grows bigger, incompatibilities must be overcome. As separate networks present the prospect of interconnection, compatibility hurdles arise. And as the pressure grows to connect all data resources together and make them universally accessible, the key technological obstacle is incompatibility.[28]

This tendency of an open space to endure, that is to diverge and differentiate, is observable from the very beginning of computer networking. With the dissemination of the results of the ARPANET experiment into the larger community of computer scientists, new types of computer network started to spring up, in a relationship of active mimesis, or innovative copying of the ARPANET model. These networks were local adaptations to different institutional demands or to diverse grassroots cultures. The development of private networks, business-oriented, grassroots, and educational, coupled with the fact that use of ARPANET was barred for a long time to institutions without Department of Defense sponsorship, initiated a movement of divergence or disjunction. By the late 1980s, although all networks adopted the basic technology of packet switching, they were also using widely different protocols and systems: Local Area Networks (LANs) based on 3COM Ethernet technologies; the academic network of Unix machines; the office networks of personal computers that used Novell file-sharing technology; the anarchic and grassroots networks of bulletin board systems; the powerful Sun workstations and the Cisco routers. To each of these networks corresponded different network architectures and cultures of use, but after the switch-over from the research network NSF to the commercial Internet in 1995 and the lifting of the ban on commercial uses, the principle of open architecture eventually allowed all these differences to connect, thus forming a single meshwork.

At a basic level, the complex operations that enable the existence of such an internetwork are managed by way of a hierarchic and modular division of labour among layers.

The functions are called layers because they are arranged in a conceptual hierarchy that proceeds from the most concrete and physical functions (such as handling electrical signals) to the most abstract functions (e.g. interpreting human-language commands by users). Each higher-level function builds on the capabilities provided by layers below.[29]

These layers go from the concrete levels of cables and wires, to communication protocols, to desktop applications such as browsers, email programs, audio-visual software, etc. Each layer also corresponds to different aspects of the government of the Internet, involving ad hoc arrangements that include professional associations of computer scientists, telecommunication companies, national governments, educational institutions, the software industry and the ISP sector. Layers can also be linked to different political economies of the Internet (from that of the telecommunication industry that looks after the telephone lines, cables and fibre optics to the software industry for desktop applications) and to different levels of technical expertise (from communication engineering to simple end-user capabilities). Innovations can thus be isolated within different layers in such a way as to keep the ripple effect of such transformations limited. In all these cases, even in the layered structure, the concern is with the propagation of differentiations and incompatibilities.

To minimize such problems, new protocols are usually inserted between systems or added to them, as an ulterior layer, without asking the current system to discard its old components and substitute them immediately with new ones. If an incompatibility emerges, it produces a 'trigger for change' requiring new technical and social negotiations. Generally, however, a new protocol or level is introduced that, by operating between or on top of different layers, will allow them all to coexist under a single common framework. This is what happened, for example, with protocols ruling the operations of gateways and routers; or with the World Wide Web; or with the X.25 protocol favoured by European telecoms companies when it was absorbed under TCP/IP. This incompatibility between different protocols, however, is never resolved once and for all, but is a recurrent and pervasive motif in the development of internetworking technologies. Incompatibility, understood as a tension between divergent moments, is not relinquished but brought into the network through a process of *horizontal addition* and/or *vertical subsumption*: a network is added to other networks; a new protocol is inserted between layers. In order to expand, an open network has to be able to extend both *upwards* and *sideways*.

Open architecture not only prescribes that internal differences should be maintained, but also that they should not be allowed to develop without an accompanying elaboration of bridging devices or protocols. A set of bodies (the Internet Architecture Board, the Internet Society and the Internet Engineering Task Force) is in charge of regularly checking that new developments do not threaten the interoperability of the medium. Different networks should thus be able to preserve an original peculiarity, but should also be monitored so that such a peculiarity would not run the risk of becoming an incompatibility.

Heterogeneity is inevitable and must be supported by design. Multiple types of hardware must be allowed for, e.g. transmission speeds differing by at least 7 orders of magnitude, various computer word lengths, and hosts ranging from memory-starved microprocessors up to massively parallel supercomputers. Multiple types of application protocol must be allowed for, ranging from the simplest such as remote login up to the most complex such as distributed databases.[30]

Network engineers argue that the internetwork was designed 'to appear seamless. Indeed they were so successful that today's Internet users probably do not even realize that their messages traverse more than one network.' Open architecture requires an active effort to build bridges between what is separated to start with and to bring together again what has diverged too far from a common line. The result is a smooth space that is infinitely crossable by flows of information detached from enclosed milieus and allowed to spread throughout an electronic maze of coaxial and fibre-optic cables and now increasingly also wireless frequencies.

It would seem reductive to read this dynamic feature of the open space of networking exclusively in terms of a technological necessity. The technical principles offer support to a tendency that is not simply inherent in the flexibility and reprogrammability of information technologies. It is almost as if the open space of internetworking was a technical solution, not only to hardware and software incompatibilities, but also to the tensions introduced by the postmodern celebration of *difference*. If, within postmodern organization theory, difference is celebrated as a positive source of added value (as in the New Labour campaign for a New Multicultural Britain in the mid 1990s), it also presents another side which constitutes a kind of underlying problematic of postmodern theory. How can difference be productively engaged with when the latter also expresses a tendency of the social to decompose into closed enclaves or identities, coexisting but not interacting with each other outside the mediation of symbols or the hostility of cultural tensions?

Within the field of information architecture, the rigidity of cultures, territories, interests, languages, and egos has been as much a material concern as has the technical incompatibility of technical machines. In the 1940s, Vannevar Bush complained that the scope and differentiation of knowledge was exceeding the rigidity of disciplinary divisions; new devices and structures were thus needed so that thinking would be able to withstand and take advantage of the exponential rise and yet specialization of knowledge. The problem arises, that is, from institutional demands for *cooperation* at the moment of emerging hegemony of immaterial labour over the mass factory mode.[31] This tendency towards the extension of the productive powers of cooperation is also present in J.C.R. Licklider's vision of an 'intergalactic' computer network as a technical expedient intended to liberate the full potential of collective thinking from the narrow boundaries of petty narcissisms and territorial attachments. For Berners-Lee, the Institute for Particle Physics (CERN) in Geneva in the 1980s was a microcosm of the globalization to come, in as much as '[p]eople brought their machines and customs with them, and everyone else just had to do their best to accommodate them. Then teams went back home and, scattered as they were across time zones and languages, still had to collaborate.'[32] From the incompatible systems and the different time zones and languages at work at CERN, Berners-Lee moved to the separate areas that constituted the Internet (email, FTP, WAIS, gopher, IRC, telnet) and subsumed them all under a new protocol, http and the URL space of the Web. In all these cases, too, we find that the technical solutions implemented to overcome the question of divergence and incompatibility start from the principle that it is both unrealistic and wasteful to think or desire that heterogeneous and divergent systems should disappear. Larry Roberts at DARPA 'viewed the diversity of computers not as an unfortunate necessity but as a strength of the system, since a network that connected the heterogeneous systems could offer users a wider range of resources'.[33] And Tim Berners-Lee realized 'that the diversity of different computer systems and networks could be a rich resource – something to be represented, not a problem to be eradicated'.[34]

This openness, then, constitutes the conditions that give rise to the most general of the political concerns expressed by a network culture. The tension between universality and divergence that informs the open space of internetworking in fact produces a rich cultural dynamics and a set of political questions that are taken up again and again across network culture at large. The history and prehistory of internetworking is thus rife with pragmatic and political questions such as: How does one avoid the openness of virtual space being overruled by its tendency to reinforce specialized interests and narrow group identities? How does one undermine the rigid lines of territorialization that divide electronic space in disconnected islands of specialized interests and firewalled domains? In this sense, Geert Lovink has rightly pointed out that Michael Hardt and Antonio Negri's popular description of network power appears to describe the space of the internetwork more accurately than it describes the political organization of global government. For Hardt and Negri, network power operates by way of a structural opening to difference and divergence, whilst being simultaneously concerned with their recuperation within the horizon of an eternal empire.

> Network power must be distinguished from other purely expansionist and imperialist forms of expansion. The fundamental difference is that the expansiveness of the immanent concept of sovereignty is inclusive, not exclusive. In other words, when it expands, this new sovereignty does not annex or destroy the other powers it faces but on the contrary opens itself to them, including them in the network.[35]

The fundamental characteristic of imperial sovereignty is that 'its space is always open'.[36] If we see the Internet as a mode of network power as described by Hardt and Negri, we have to count as a dimension of its openness not only a benevolent welcoming of differences but also a more general drive towards expansion. The Internet is an expansive and imperial medium, not in the sense that the number of connected users is bound to increase (we cannot know the events that will shape the future), but more in terms of an active openness of network spatiality. There is nothing to stop every object from being given an Internet address that makes it locatable in electronic space. Every object and device can, in principle, be networked to the network of networks in a kind of ubiquitous computational landscape (as described by Bill Gates for example in his vision of the home of the future). At the same time, the addition of new networks (of objects, devices, machines and people) does not leave its space unaffected but involves the whole duration of the network. An outcome of this tendency to acentered interoperability is that the topological and dynamical features of the Internet suggest a much more complex picture than that of a single, electronic space–time – linking the local and the global according to a mode of simultaneous interaction or tele-command. At the same time, the general notion of an open space subjected to the double tension between compatibility and divergence still leaves us with a very generic understanding of network duration. What is this dynamic movement that network architecture both produces and attempts to contain? And what is its relationship to the political and cultural questions raised above about the microphysics of the internetwork topology?

FRINGE INTELLIGENCE

Temporalization penetrates the machine from all sides, the emergence of a machine marks a date, a change, different from a structural representation.[37]

To say that sociologists and cultural theorists have tended to overlook the duration of electronic space does not mean that the study of network dynamics is a neglected field. While sociologists and philosophers have thoroughly debated the relation between space and time in network societies, mathematicians and physicists have been busy modelling the dynamics of Internet traffic and its relation to the topology of cyberspace. What the former mostly see as a single electronic space causing a space–time implosion, the latter see as the epiphenomenal manifestation of hidden physical laws that make the Internet part of a more general class of biophysical systems. On the one hand, a technology implicated in the social collapse of distances, the imperialist homogenization of times, and the reduction of the heterogeneity of the world to the one dimension of communication; on the other hand, a type of dynamical physical system characterized by a specific topological distribution, whose laws must be discovered and formalized. In between these different visions of the network lies the sprawl of Internet culture – with its vast digital archives, its mutating landscape of search engines and corporate pages, networked home pages, mailing lists, electronic newsletters, blogs and wikis, news sites and newsletters, spam and porn, peer-to-peer networking, bulletin board, chatlines and ICQ. Between the scientific search for laws and the sociological need to name macro-shifts in social experience, the transversal line of culture suggests another way of framing the problem.

The bewildering variety and dynamism of cultural expression on the Internet has often been understood as an effect of a new mode of communication (distributed and many-to-many rather than centralized and few-to-many). If we consider the technical form of the media, one of the basic ways in which this network of networks differs from the mass media system is that it does not operate by synchronizing a closed space of receivers around a single or limited number of frequencies so that a particular message flow can be streamed from a central point (involving a handful of broadcasters) to the margins (involving a segmented multiplicity of viewers). If modern communication organizes space by the principle whereby messages are beamed linearly to a segmented and privatized social space, distributed communication breaks this model down at the receiver level as well as at the level of the message itself.

One of the major points of departure that distinguishes the Internet from other modern decentralized media (from telegraphy to radio) is that messages are not beamed or transmitted through a channel, but broken down and let loose in the network to find their destination. There is mostly no straight line connecting a point *A* to a point *B*, but a multiplicity of potential routes through which data packets have to find their ways. The packet-switching mode contributes to a peculiar quality of information flow within the internetwork: a diffuse and chaotic movement marked by gradients of openness and closure. This feature of the movement of information through the internetwork is probably the most mythologized of all the technical aspects of the Internet, at least since the day when John Gilmore suggested that 'the Internet treats censorship as damage and routes around it'. It is at the basis of the notion that the Internet is in principle uncensorable and endowed with its own vitality.

Particularly important among the contributions of ARPANET researchers to the emergence of a new electronic space freed of the limitations of isolated computers was their demonstration of the feasibility of Paul Baran's vision of a packet-switched network.[38] As is well known, Paul Baran argued for two features of such networks: messages should be broken down into equally sized packets, enveloped by an electronic tag carrying information about the sender's and receiver's addresses and the position of the packet within the overall message; and they should be sent out on their own to find their destination in the best possible way by travelling from node to node. In other words, in a packet-switched network messages are fragmented, divided into packets, and sent off into the big wide network to find the quickest way to their destination.

This mode of communication was initially deemed unsuitable for voice networks, because telephonic conversations need the continuous use of a line in order to carry the high information content of the voice. In the light of the technical limitations of the 1950s and 1960s, when the model was devised, to packet-switch a telephone conversation or to break down the voice into several packets would have involved substantial corruption in the quality of information. Thus telephone conversations required a 'circuit switching' approach that opens up and reserves a line for the whole duration of the conversation (circuit switching of early telephony was entrusted to the figure of the telephone operator, usually a young woman). Information traffic among computers, on the other hand, tended to happen in bursts, and this left a considerable amount of bandwidth unused. Baran thought that by implementing a packet-switching network, bandwidth could be more effectively managed and made full use of. If a line was not used for a while, then it could be used by other packets looking for all possible places of passage in their search for their destination. Significantly, Baran proposed that a packet-switched network should be digital, in as much as analogue signals would lose quality once submitted to the lengthy relay journey of data packets in packet-switched mode. Unlike telegraphy and telephony, then, the communication of information in computer networks does not start with a sender, a receiver and a line, but with an overall information space, constituted by a tangle of possible directions and routes, where information propagates by autonomously finding the lines of least resistance. Messages are broken down into packets and each packet is sent out into the network to find its destination by being relayed around through a network of autonomous and decentralized nodes. If any obstacles arise along the main lines, the various packets can be sent out in different directions to find their own best possible routes. Messages are broken down so as to be able to maximize the communication capacity of telephone lines, avoid interference and accidental or deliberate obstructions and ruptures in the communication flow.

The space of communication is thus radically modified: yes, there are still messages being transmitted, but the messages are broken down and granted a kind of autonomous movement. The linearity which channelled the turbulent flow of information in the modern media is supplemented by another principle, where there are not so much senders, channels and receivers, as nodes, relays and packets, all lying flat within a space of more or less open, or obstructed, flow. If a node is blocked, the packet or datagram is sent off to a different node, which in its turn will pass it on until the shortest possible route is found. This shortest possible route, however, is variable and overall dependent on the traffic and usage of the network.

While the distributed movement of packets holds a key position within the mythology of the self-organizing Internet, the other corollary of packet switching (fringe intelligence) is less remarked upon but equally important. In a distributed network, we do not have a relation between aerials and transmitters, but among an assembage of semi-autonomous nodes that are programmed with a kind of basic intelligence. As the Network Working Group put it, the intelligence is end to end.[39] This is a pragmatic choice in as much as a traffic of the magnitude and nonlinear complexity of that crossing computer networks on a daily basis cannot operate without distributing the responsibility to the end systems themselves.

> A specific case is that any network, however carefully designed, will be subject to failures of transmission at some statistically determined rate. The best way to cope with this is to accept it, and give responsibility for the integrity of communication to the end systems.[40]

It is this delegation of responsibility to the margins, or fringe intelligence, that is, so to speak, the technical engine on which the tendency to divergence can ride. In Baran's model each node should be able to select the quickest route from *A* to *B* (the line of least resistance), but it should also record this route in its routing tables, in order to maximize the transmission rate. When another node is taken down, each node should be able to 'forget' that node and that route; find and remember a new one; and update its routing tables for next time. In this way, for Baran the network should be able to survive the destruction of up to 50 per cent of its nodes, after which even a distributed network would be hard-pressed to recover. Electronic space is made adaptive through the selective introduction of a 'network memory', capable of remembering and forgetting in relation to the perception that nodes have of the network at any given moment. 'What is envisioned is a network of unmanned digital switches implementing a self-learning policy at each node so that overall traffic is effectively routed in a changing environment ... without need for a central and possibly vulnerable control point.'[41] The combination of packet switching, end-to-end intelligence and routing makes computer networks a kind of distributed neural network able to remember and forget. This fringe intelligence produces a space that is not just a 'space of passage' for information, but an informational machine itself – an active and turbulent space. This quality of informational space makes the Internet a space suitable to the spread of contagion and transversal propagation of movement (from computer viruses to ideas and affects).

In a packet-switched network, then, there is no simple vector or route between *A* (for example a computer in Taiwan) and *B* (a computer in Cape Town). Even as such space is perceived as simultaneous from the point of view of the subjects engaged in receiving and sending messages in real time from all over the world, that does not imply an actual simultaneity – as if the whole of the electronic space were a blank support for the transmission of messages. Beneath the level of desktop applications such as browsers and email, the space of the internetwork is continuously although unevenly agitated, constrained and transformed by the movement of packets. The route which a message might take has to take into account at all points the overall traffic of the network, the points of blockages, the local catastrophes, political repressions, cultures of secrecies, the blind alleys and the open channels. The various cultural formations and forces that over the years have engaged with the medium have enthusiastically taken over this feature of network space and made of it a fundamental aspect of its overall culture. This movement is the condition within which Internet culture operates and it constitutes an important interface with the world of locality. The relation between local and global, the territory and the network is thus that of fluctuation, of an increased or decreased, obstructed or relayed flow.

The layered structure of the Internet emerges, so to speak, as a system of channels and microchannels that can structure such basic turbulent flow. As we have seen, the nonlinear movement of information does not produce a random and homogeneous informational milieu, but it is given form and organized by semiotic economies, client–server relationships, local points of centralization, and international boards in charge of monitoring and assessing the viability of its technical protocols to the massive scaling process undergone by the medium at different stages of its short history. The nonlinear movement of information, then, makes the Internet not so much a unified electronic grid as a chaotic informational milieu – whether it is about the movement of email, the diffusion of viruses, the constitution of ad hoc communication arrangements (such as mirror sites for sites that are censored) or the periodic surfacing and disappearance of pirate islands of connectivity (as for example in 'warez' or pirate software sites).[42] It is here that the practices of appearance and disappearance, assembling and dismantling, forwarding and deleting unfold within a veritable informational ecology of viruses and parasites, petitions and cries for help, scams and junk mails. There is no cultural experimentation with aesthetic forms or political organization, no building of alliances or elaboration of tactics that does not have to confront the turbulence of electronic space.[43] The politics of network culture are thus not only about competing viewpoints, anarchic self-regulation and barriers to access, but also about the pragmatic production of viable topological formations able to persist within an open and fluid milieu.

Internet culture has thus given us some important topoi of network space, able to capture and impart a specific speed and consistency to the potential indeterminacy of information flows. We have had boards and domains, lists and webs, but also spheres and rings binding local areas of connectivity within an open information space. These figures express the power of a local movement able to bind the turbulence of the flows within a new type of informational structure. If bulletin board systems offered a steady platform from which to launch oneself into an open info-space, the fragmentation of web space that favours the power of attraction of the portals is counteracted by web rings, where small sites with similar content form a circular vortex able to capture and channel the attention of the web surfer. The sphere has also been used as another model for the multidimensional aggregation of web rings, or simply as a way to designate a kind of informational gravitation around a common orbit. The term 'blogosphere' for example designates the ways in which all the personal web logs, or hyperlinked online journals, can be considered as ultimately related to each other within the informational orbit of the blogging movement.[44] These figures are traced not so much by a link connecting two different sites across the grid of a common domain name, as by transversal movements, continuously spilling out of the grid, constituting the network as a space of centripetal and centrifugal movements, of spirals and vortexes, in various overall states of contraction and dilation.

While the topology of the web maintains a certain level of solidity that makes the notion of rings and spheres appropriate, the overall space of the internetwork is also crossed by vortical movements that betray a microscopic fluidity and instability – informed by the power of rippling centrifugal and centripetal forces. A network microphysics is also made of temporary and unstable alliances and relations – such as the temporary chat channels that are opened up and closed down for the duration of a conversation or the fleeting email contacts that randomly link distant and even opposed areas of network space.

These figures and contacts involve a crucial experimentation with the peculiar semi-fluid mechanics of network space at large. Internet forms such as list servers and majordomo lists actively experiment with such instability to build vortical structures able to combine permanence and impermanence, dynamism and consistency. A successful mailing list has to be able to exercise enough of a pull on its members and the material circulated so as to keep a certain level of consistency and dynamism, durability and renewal.[45] It opens up the political model of the 'group' with its tendency to sectarianism and infighting to an open informational milieu. The production of collective modes of organization (from a 'group' to 'collaborative filtering' and 'collective intelligence') requires not only a knowledge of social and psychological dynamics informing a collective mode of production, but also an active engagement with the larger ecology of the Internet – screening out the junk, balancing the passive energy of the lurkers with the hyperactivism of the regular posters and keeping the vandals out.[46] The history of the Internet is littered with failed experiments in network hydrodynamics, vortexes that dissolved under the tides of the network. We can only mention here a few classic stories of centripetal dissolution: Alluquère Rosanne Stone's CommuniTree, a 1980s community bulletin board eventually dismantled by the charge of hordes of teenage hackers;[47] Inke Arns and Andreas Broeckmann's activist list Syndicate, done in by net parasites and anti-censorship campaigners;[48] and other classic examples of community networks being pulled apart by powerful economic forces, such as Howard Rheingold's Electric Mind, Amsterdam's public Digital City project and the famous net-art list 'rhizome'. Each of these cases expresses a specificity which needs to be analysed in its own particular circumstances (thus for CommuniTree the problem was that of the immaturity of cyberculture; for the Digital City it was the dot-com wave that proved to be too much; and so on). However, overall, we can claim that what all these examples share is the fact that for a while they maintained a precarious balance between centripetal and centrifugal forces which allowed them to prosper in spite of what Phil Agre has called 'the always imminent threat of heat death' that befalls all those informational experiments that are unable to deal with the entropic dynamics of the network milieu.[49]

This difficult balancing act is obviously far from being an exclusive feature of the Internet (indeed in as much as the informational dimension crosses all communication spaces we might use a similar model to analyse the emergence and disapperance of cultural formations as such). On the other hand, it is within a culture of internetworked, informational and distributed communication that the dynamics through which cultural assemblages are formed explicitly becomes the condition for a kind of network micropolitics. Any local, that is bounded, cultural phenomenon within the network is always caught on one side by the danger of being overwhelmed by the open network ecology; and on the other side by that of solidifying to the point of becoming a self-contained and self-referential archipelago of the like-minded (and hence succumbing to a kind of heat death). On the other hand, this mobility of cyberspace can also be productively exploited – hackers have tuned the art of forming and deforming cyberspace to a fine degree. Warez boards offering pirate software, for example, are particular evanescent and mobile informational islands, appearing and disappearing, springing out of nowhere, signalled only to insiders, only to dissolve as soon as the frantic transactions are carried out.

We also need to emphasize that while these centripetal and centrifugal movements are central to the evolution of electronic space, they do not take place within an isolated and self-referential infosphere. On the contrary, they are related to the overall informational dimension that cuts across the global matrix of communication of which the Internet is part. As an open space, the Internet is open not only to the addition of new nodes, but also to the informational flows relayed by television, radio and popular culture, as well as by political passions involving social antagonisms and conflicts. The centripetal/centrifugal movements that determine the fate of informational cultures are open to the overall plane of communication, and as such the Internet can also be said to be characterized by another duration, that which relates it to the various states of contraction and dilation experienced by the global communication system.

The openness of the Internet in relation to the network matrix of which it is a part was foregrounded, for example, in the wake of the attacks on the World Trade Center on 11 September 2001. If 9/11 was at some level a quintessential televisual global event, it also brought to light some of the dynamic features of the overall configuration of communication that links in a relationship of resonance or direct interconnection a multiplicity of media outlets and communication devices. The attacks, in fact, famously brought the Internet to a state of virtual standstill. It was not simply that they destroyed a key communication centre located underneath the Twin Towers, but that they also provoked an unprecedented and simultaneous use of the Internet as a way of gathering news, contacting friends and acquaintances, or simply exchanging reactions and opinions. This synchronized assault on bandwidth did not so much paralyse the network as contract it – at first towards the great Internet portals, but successively also in a dense transversal traffic of news and commentary, direct reporting and critical interventions, of new web pages and web logs, an activity that whipped the Internet into a kind of electronic frenzy. The network, that is, is not a closed electronic space, but it is literally contracted by the intensity of the informational flows that reach it from the outside, an intensity which rises and declines, disperses and diversifies again to the rhythms of the geopolitical events, social debates and cultural trends that are the whole onto which a network duration opens.[50]

AFTERTHOUGHT

When looking at the socio-technical organization of information operated by Internet protocols, it is difficult not to be struck by how a military and scientific technology has come to model so well a fractal and turbulent mode of globalization that exceeds on all sides the early rhetoric of immateriality and timelessness. The polarity between levels of universality and movements of differentiation that concerned network architects and engineers mirrors that of a process of globalization that beneath the shadow cast by neo-imperial formations is similarly striving for some kind of pragmatic politics able to conjugate such tendencies within a common, constitutive movement. The tension arising out of the incompatibilities and divergences produced by pre-existing differences *and* an ongoing process of differentiation becomes a tendency towards the production of new structures that temporarily resolve some of the incompatibilities at stake. But in a way, we can say that the whole plane of network culture is crossed by social undercurrents that pose the problem of a global geopolitics not only at the level of a technical infrastructure, but, more importantly, at the speed of cultural and informational flows. A network culture can never be a unitary formation, describing a homogeneity of practices across a global communication matrix. On the contrary, if such a thing exists, it can only describe the dynamics informing the cultural and political process of recomposition and decomposition of a highly differentiated, multi-scaled and yet common global network culture.

3
Free Labour[1]

The real *not-capital* is *labour.*
(Karl Marx *Grundrisse*)

Working in the digital media industry was never as much fun as it was made out to be. Certainly, for the workers of the best-known and most highly valued companies, work might have been a brief experience of something that did not feel like work at all.[2] On the other hand, even during the dot-com boom the 'netslaves' of the homonymous webzine had always been vociferous about the shamelessly exploitative nature of the job, its punishing work rhythms and its ruthless casualization.[3] They talked about '24/7 electronic sweatshops', complained about the 90-hour week and the 'moronic management of new media companies'. Antagonism in the new media industry also affected the legions of volunteers running well-known sites for the Internet giants. In early 1999, seven of the 15,000 'volunteers' of America Online rocked the info-loveboat by asking the Department of Labor to investigate whether AOL owed them back wages for the years of playing chat hosts for free.[4] They used to work long hours and love it; but they also felt the pain of being burned by digital media.

These events pointed to an inevitable backlash against the glamorization of digital labour, which highlighted its continuities with the modern sweatshop and the increasing degradation of knowledge work. Yet the question of labour in a 'digital economy' as an innovative development of the familiar logic of capitalist exploitation is not so easily dismissed. The netslaves are not simply a typical form of labour on the Internet; they also embody a complex relation to labour, which is widespread in late capitalist societies.

In this chapter, we call this excessive activity that makes the Internet a thriving and hyperactive medium 'free labour' – a feature of the cultural economy at large, and an important, yet unacknowledged, source of value in advanced capitalist societies. By looking at the Internet as a specific instance of the fundamental role played by free labour, we will also highlight the connections between the 'digital

73

economy' and what the Italian autonomists have called the 'social factory' (or 'society–factory').[5] The 'society–factory' describes a process whereby 'work processes have shifted from the factory to society, thereby setting in motion a truly complex machine'.[6] Simultaneously voluntarily given and unwaged, enjoyed and exploited, free labour on the Net includes the activity of building web sites, modifying software packages, reading and participating in mailing lists and building virtual spaces. Far from being an 'unreal', empty space, the Internet is animated by cultural and technical labour through and through, a continuous production of value which is completely immanent in the flows of the network society at large.

Support for this argument, however, is immediately complicated by the recent history of Anglo-American cultural theory. How should we speak of labour, especially cultural and technical labour, after the demolition job carried out by 30 years of postmodernism? The postmodern socialist feminism of Donna Haraway's 'Cyborg Manifesto' spelled out some of the reasons behind the antipathy of 1980s critical theory for Marxist analyses of labour. Haraway explicitly rejected the humanistic tendencies of theorists who see the latter as the 'pre-eminently privileged category enabling the Marxist to overcome illusion and find that point of view which is necessary for changing the world'.[7] Paul Gilroy similarly expressed his discontent at the inadequacy of the Marxist analysis of labour to the descendants of slaves, who value artistic expression as 'the means towards both individual self-fashioning and communal liberation'.[8] If labour is 'the humanizing activity that makes [white] man', then, surely, this 'humanising' labour does not really belong in the age of networked, posthuman intelligence.

However, the 'informatics of domination' which Haraway describes in the 'Manifesto' is certainly preoccupied with the relation between technology, labour and capital. In the 20 years since its publication, this triangulation has become even more evident. The expansion of the Internet has given ideological and material support to contemporary trends towards increased flexibility of the workforce, continuous reskilling, freelance work, and the diffusion of practices such as 'supplementing' (bringing supplementary work home from the conventional office).[9] Advertising campaigns and business manuals suggest that the Internet is not only a site of disintermediation (embodying the famous death of the middle man, from bookshops to travel agencies and computer stores), but also the means through which a flexible, collective network intelligence has come into being.

I will not offer here a judgement on the 'effects' of the Internet on society. What I will rather do is map the way in which the Internet connects to the autonomist 'social factory'. We will look, that is, at how the 'outernet' – the network of social, cultural and economic relationships which criss-crosses and exceeds the Internet – surrounds and connects the latter to larger flows of labour, culture and power. It is fundamental to move beyond the notion that cyberspace is about escaping reality in order to understand how the reality of the Internet is deeply connected to the development of late postindustrial societies as a whole. It is related to phenomena that have been defined as 'external economies' within theoretical pespectives (such as the theory of transaction costs) suggesting that 'the production of value is increasingly involving the capture of productive elements and social wealth that are *outside* the direct productive process ...'.[10] Cultural and technical work is central to the Internet but is also a widespread activity throughout advanced capitalist societies. Such labour is not exclusive to so-called 'knowledge workers', but is a pervasive feature of the postindustrial economy. The pervasiveness of such diffuse cultural production questions the legitimacy of a fixed distinction between production and consumption, labour and culture. It also undermines Gilroy's distinction between work as 'servitude, misery and subordination' and artistic expression as the means to self-fashioning and communal liberation. The increasingly blurred territory between production and consumption, work and cultural expression, however, does not signal the recomposition of the alienated Marxist worker. The Internet does not automatically turn every user into an active producer, and every worker into a creative subject. The process whereby production and consumption are reconfigured within the category of free labour signals the unfolding of another logic of value, whose operations need careful analysis.[11]

THE DIGITAL ECONOMY

The term 'digital economy' emerged in the late 1990s as a way to summarize some of the processes described above. As a term, it seems to describe a formation which intersects on the one hand with the postmodern cultural economy (the media, the university and the arts) and on the other hand with the information industry (the information and communication complex). Such an intersection of two different fields of production constitutes a challenge to a theoretical and practical engagement with the question of labour, a question which has become marginal for media studies as compared with questions of ownership (within political economy) and consumption (within cultural studies).

We will distinguish here between the New Economy, 'a historical period marker [that] acknowledges its conventional association with Internet companies',[12] and the digital economy – a less transient phenomenon based on key features of digitized information (its ease of copying and low or zero cost of sharing). In Richard Barbrook's definition, the digital economy is characterized by the emergence of new technologies (computer networks) and new types of worker (such as digital artisans).[13] According to Barbrook, the digital economy is a mixed economy: it includes a public element (the state's funding of the original research that produced ARPANET, the financial support to academic activities which had a substantial role in shaping the culture of the Internet); a market-driven element (a latecomer that tries to appropriate the digital economy by reintroducing commodification); and a gift economy (the true expression of the cutting edge of capitalist production which prepares its eventual overcoming into a future 'anarcho-communism').

What Barbrook proposed was that the vision of politicians and corporate leaders who linked the future of capitalism to the informational commodity involved a basic misunderstanding. Pointing to the world of discussion groups, mailing lists and the distributed learning of programmers, he suggested that the Internet was far from simply being a new way to sell commodities. The predominance of relationships of collaboration across distance and exchange without money suggested that this was a practised relationship with a viable and alternative political and economic model.

> Unrestricted by physical distance, they collaborate with each other without the direct mediation of money and politics. Unconcerned about copyright, they give and receive information without thought of payment. In the absence of states or markets to mediate social bonds, network communities are instead formed through the mutual obligations created by gifts of time and ideas.[14]

Barbrook's vision of the informational commons was only reinforced by the subsequent explosion of peer-to-peer, file-sharing networks – a huge network phenomenon that had the music and film industry up in arms.

From a Marxist–Hegelian angle, Barbrook saw the high-tech gift economy as a process of overcoming capitalism from the inside. The high-tech gift economy is a pioneering moment which transcends both the purism of the New Left do-it-yourself culture and the neoliberalism of the free-market ideologues: 'money–commodity and gift relations are not just in conflict with each other, but also co-exist in symbiosis.'[15] Participants in the gift economy are not reluctant to use market resources and government funding to pursue a potlatch economy of free exchange. However, the potlatch and the economy ultimately remain irreconcilable, and the market economy is always threatening to reprivatize the common enclaves of the gift economy. Commodification, the reimposition of a regime of property, is, in Barbrook's opinion, the main strategy through which capitalism tries to bring back the anarcho-communism of the Net into its fold.

This early attempt to offer a polemical platform from which to think about the digital economy overemphasized the autonomy of the high-tech gift economy from capitalism. The processes of exchange which characterize the Internet are not simply the re-emergence of communism within the cutting edge of the economy, a repressed other which resurfaces just at the moment when communism seems defeated. It is important to remember that the gift economy, as part of a larger informational economy, is itself an important force within the reproduction of the labour force in late capitalism as a whole. The provision of 'free labour', as we shall see later, is a fundamental moment in the creation of value in the economy at large – beyond the digital economy of the Internet. As will be made clear, the conditions that make free labour an important element of the digital economy are based on a difficult, experimental compromise between the historically rooted cultural and affective desire for creative production (of the kind more commonly associated with Gilroy's emphasis on 'individual self-fashioning and communal liberation') and the current capitalist emphasis on knowledge as the main source of added value.

The volunteers for America On Line, the netslaves and the amateur web designers did not work only because capital wanted them to, but they were acting out a desire for affective and cultural production which was none the less real just because it was socially shaped.

The cultural, technical and creative work which supported the New Economy had been made possible by the development of capital beyond the early industrial and Fordist modes of production and therefore is particularly abundant in those areas where post-Fordism has been at work for several decades. In the overdeveloped countries, the end of the factory has spelled out the marginalisation of the old working class, but it has also produced generations of workers who have been repeatedly addressed as active consumers of meaningful commodities. Free labour is the moment where this knowledgeable consumption of culture is translated into excess productive activities that are pleasurably embraced and at the same time often shamelessly exploited.

Management theory has also been increasingly concerned with the question of knowledge work, that indefinable quality which is essential to the processes of stimulating innovation and achieving the goals of competitiveness. For example, Don Tapscott, in a classic example of New Economy managerial literature, *The Digital Economy*, wrote about a 'new economy based on the networking of human intelligence'.[16] Human intelligence provides the much needed added value, which is essential to the economic health of the organization. Human intelligence, however, also poses a problem: it cannot be managed in quite the same way as more traditional types of labour. Knowledge workers need open organizational structures in order to produce, because the production of knowledge is rooted in collaboration; this is what Barbrook had defined as the 'gift economy'.

> ... the concept of supervision and management is changing to team-based structures. Anyone responsible for managing knowledge workers know they cannot be 'managed' in the traditional sense. Often they have specialized knowledge and skills that cannot be matched or even understood by management. A new challenge to management is first to attract and retain these assets by marketing the organization to them, and second *to provide the creative and open communications environment where such workers can effectively apply and enhance their knowledge.*[17]

For Tapscott, therefore, the digital economy magically resolves the contradictions of industrial societies, such as class struggle: whereas in the industrial economy the 'worker tried to achieve fulfillment through leisure [and]... was alienated from the means of production which were owned and controlled by someone else', in the digital economy the worker achieves fulfillment through work and finds in her brain her own, unalienated means of production.[18] Such means of production need to be cultivated by encouraging the worker to participate in a culture of exchange, whose flows are mainly kept within the company but also need to involve an 'outside', a contact with the fast-moving world of knowledge in general. The convention, the exhibition and the conference – the traditional ways of supporting this general exchange – are supplemented by network technologies both inside and outside the company. Although the traffic of these flows of knowledge needs to be monitored (hence the corporate concerns about the use of intranets), the Internet effectively functions as a channel through which 'human intelligence' renews its capacity to produce.

Is it possible to look beyond the totalizing hype of the managerial literature, but also beyond some of the conceptual limits of Barbrook's gift economy model? We will look at some possible explanations for the coexistence, within the debate about the digital economy, of discourses which see it as an oppositional movement and others which see it as a functional development to new mechanisms of extraction of value. Is the end of Marxist alienation wished for by the management guru the same thing as the gift economy heralded by leftist discourse?

We can start undoing this deadlock by subtracting the label 'digital economy' from its exclusive anchorage within advanced forms of labour (we can start, then, by de-pioneering it). This chapter describes the 'digital economy' as a specific mechanism of internal 'capture' of larger pools of social and cultural knowledge. The digital economy is an important area of experimentation with value and free cultural/ affective labour. It is about specific forms of production (web design, multimedia production, digital services and so on), but it is also about forms of labour we do not immediately recognize as such: chat, real-life stories, mailing lists, amateur newsletters and so on. These types of cultural and technical labour are not produced by capitalism in any direct, cause-and-effect fashion, that is they have not developed simply as an answer to the economic needs of capital. However, they have developed in relation to the expansion of the cultural industries and they are part of a process of economic experimentation with the creation of monetary value out of knowledge/culture/affect.

This process is different from that described by popular, left-wing wisdom about the incorporation of authentic cultural moments: it is not, then, about the bad boys of capital moving in on underground subcultures or subordinate cultures and 'incorporating' the fruits of their production (styles, languages, music) into the media food chain. This process is usually considered the end of a particular cultural formation, or at least the end of its 'authentic' phase. After incorporation, local cultures are picked up and distributed globally, thus contributing to cultural hybridization or cultural imperialism (depending on whom you listen to). Rather than capital 'incorporating' from the outside the authentic fruits of the collective imagination, it seems more reasonable to think of cultural flows as originating within a field which is always and already capitalism. Incorporation is not about capital descending on authentic culture, but a more immanent process of channelling of collective labour (even as cultural labour) into monetary flows and its structuration within capitalist business practices.

Subcultural movements have stuffed the pockets of multinational capitalism for decades. Nurtured by the consumption of earlier cultural moments, subcultures have provided the look, style and sounds that sell clothes, CDs, video games, films and advertising slots on television. This has often happened through the active participation of subcultural members in the production of cultural goods (independent labels in music; small designer shops in fashion).[19] This participation is, as the word suggests, a voluntary phenomenon, although it is regularly accompanied by cries of 'Sell-out!' The fruits of collective cultural labour have been not simply appropriated, but voluntarily *channelled* and controversially *structured* within capitalist business practices. The relation between culture, the cultural industry and labour in these movements is much more complex than the notion of incorporation suggests. In this sense, the digital economy is not a new phenomenon, but simply a new phase of this longer history of experimentation.

KNOWLEDGE CLASS AND IMMATERIAL LABOUR

In spite of the numerous, more or less disingenuous endorsements of the democratic potential of the Internet, its links with capitalism have always been a bit too tight for comfort to concerned political minds. It has been very tempting to counteract the naive technological utopianism by pointing out how computer networks are the material and ideological heart of informated capital. The Internet advertised on television and portrayed by the print media seems not just the latest incarnation of capital's inexhaustible search for new markets, but also a full consensus-creating machine, which socializes the mass of proletarianized knowledge workers into the economy of continuous innovation.[20] After all, if we do not get online soon, the hype suggests, we will become obsolete, unnecessary, disposable. If we do, we are promised, we will become part of the 'hive mind', the immaterial economy of networked, intelligent subjects in charge of speeding up the rhythms of capital's 'incessant waves of branching innovations'.[21] Multimedia artists, writers, journalists, software programmers, graphic designers and activists, together with small and large companies, are at the core of this project. For some they are the cultural elite, for others a new form of proletarianized labour.[22] Accordingly, digital workers are described as resisting or supporting the project of capital, often in direct relation to their positions in the networked, horizontal and yet hierarchical world of knowledge work.

Any judgement on the political potential of the Internet, then, is tied not only to its much vaunted capacity to allow decentralized access to information, but also to the question of who uses the Internet and how. If the decentralized structure of the Net is to count for anything at all, the argument goes, then we need to know about its constituent population (hence the endless statistics about income, nationality, gender and race of Internet users, the most polled, probed and yet opaque survey material in the world). If this population is still largely made up of 'knowledge workers', a global elite with no ties to a disenfranchised majority, then it matters whether these are seen as the owners of elitist cultural and economic power or the avant-garde of new configurations of labour which do not automatically guarantee elite status.

The question of who uses the Internet is both necessary and yet misleading. It is necessary because we have to ask who is participating in the digital economy before we can pass a judgement on the latter. It is misleading because it implies that all we need to know is how to locate the knowledge workers within a 'class', and knowing which class it is will give us an answer to the political potential of the Net as a whole. If we can prove that knowledge workers are the avant-garde of labour, then the Net becomes a site of resistance;[23] if we can prove that knowledge workers wield the power in informated societies, then the Net is an extended gated community for the middle classes.[24] Even admitting that knowledge workers are indeed fragmented in terms of hierarchy and status won't help us that much; it will still lead to a simple system of categorization, in which the

Net becomes a field of struggle between the diverse constituents of the knowledge class.

The question is further complicated by the stubborn resistance of 'knowledge' to quantification: knowledge cannot be exclusively pinned down to specific social segments. Although the shift from factory to office work, from production to services, is widely acknowledged, it just isn't clear why some people qualify and some others do not.[25] The 'knowledge worker' is a very contested sociological category.

A more interesting move is possible, however, by not looking for the knowledge class within quantifiable parameters but by concentrating instead on 'labour'. Although the notion of class retains a material value which is indispensable to make sense of the experience of concrete historical subjects, it also has its limits: for example it 'freezes' the subject, just like a substance within the chemical periodical table – one is born as a certain element (working class metal) but then might become something else (middle class silicon) if submitted to the proper alchemical processes (education and income). Such an understanding of class also freezes out the flows of culture and money which mobilize the labour force as a whole. In terms of Internet use, it gives rise to the generalized endorsements and condemnations which I have described above and does not explain or make sense of the heterogeneity and yet commonalties of Internet users. It seems therefore more useful to think in terms of what the Italian autonomists, and especially Maurizio Lazzarato, have described as *immaterial labour*. For Lazzarato, the concept of immaterial labour refers to *two different aspects* of labour:

> On the one hand, as regards the 'informational content' of the commodity, it refers directly to the changes taking place in workers' labor processes ... where the skills involved in direct labor are increasingly skills involving cybernetics and computer control (and horizontal and vertical communication). On the other hand, as regards the activity that produces the 'cultural content' of the commodity, immaterial labor involves a series of activities that are not normally recognized as 'work' – in other words, the kinds of activities involved in defining and fixing cultural and artistic standards, fashions, tastes, consumer norms, and, more strategically, public opinion.[26]

Immaterial labour, unlike the knowledge worker, is not completely confined to a specific class formation. Lazzarato insists that this form of labour power is not limited to highly skilled workers, but is a form of activity of every productive subject within postindustrial societies. In the highly skilled worker, these capacities are already there. In the young worker, however, the 'precarious worker', and the unemployed youth, these capacities are 'virtual', that is they are there but are still undetermined. This means that immaterial labour is a virtuality (an undetermined capacity) which belongs to the postindustrial productive subjectivity as a whole. For example, the obsessive emphasis on education of 1990s governments can be read as an attempt to stop this virtuality from disappearing or from being channelled into places which would not be as acceptable to the current power structures. In spite of all the contradictions of advanced capital and its relation to structural unemployment, postmodern governments do not like the completely unemployable. The potentialities of work must be kept alive, the unemployed must undergo continuous training in order to be both monitored and kept alive as some kind of postindustrial reserve force. Nor can they be allowed to channel their energy into the experimental, nomadic, and antiproductive lifestyles which in Britain have been so savagely attacked by the Criminal Justice Act since the mid 1990s.[27]

However, unlike the post-Fordists, and in accordance with his autonomist origins, Lazzarato does not conceive of immaterial labour as purely functional to a new historical phase of capitalism:

> The virtuality of this capacity is neither empty nor ahistoric; it is rather an opening and a potentiality, that have as their historical origins and antecedents the 'struggle against work' of the Fordist worker and, in more recent times, the processes of socialization, educational formation, and cultural self-valorization.[28]

This dispersal of immaterial labour (as a virtuality and an actuality) problematizes the idea of the 'knowledge worker' as a class in the 'industrial' sense of the word. As a collective quality of the labour force, immaterial labour can be understood to pervade the social body with different degrees of intensity. This intensity is produced by the processes of 'channelling' of the capitalist formation which distributes value according to its logic of profit.[29] If knowledge is inherently collective, this is even more the case in the postmodern cultural economy: music, fashion, and information are all produced collectively but are selectively compensated. Only some companies are picked up by corporate distribution chains in the case of fashion and music; only a few sites are invested in by venture capital. However it is a form of collective cultural labour which makes these products possible even though the profit is disproportionately appropriated by established corporations.

From this point of view, the well-known notion that the Internet materializes a 'collective intelligence' is not completely off the mark. The Internet highlights the existence of networks of immaterial labour and speeds up their accretion into a collective entity. The productive capacities of immaterial labour on the Internet encompass the work of writing/reading/managing and participating in mailing lists/websites/chat lines. These activities fall outside the concept of 'abstract labour', which Marx defined as the provision of time for the production of value regardless of the useful qualities of the product.[30] They witness an investment of desire into production of the kind cultural theorists have mainly theorized in relation to consumption.

This explosion of productive activities was undermined for various commentators by the globally privileged character of the Internet population. However, we might also argue that to recognize the existence of immaterial labour as a diffuse, collective quality of postindustrial labour in its entirety does not deny the existence of hierarchies of knowledge (both technical and cultural) which pre-structure (but do not determine) the nature of such activities. These hierarchies shape the degrees to which such virtualities become actualities, that is they go from being potential to being realized as processual, constituting moments of cultural, affective, and technical production. Neither capital nor living labour want a labour force which is permanently excluded from the possibilities of immaterial labour. But this is where their desires cease to coincide. Capital wants to retain control over the unfolding of these virtualities and the processes of valorization. The relative abundance of cultural/technical/affective production on the Net, then, does not exist as a free-floating postindustrial utopia but in full, mutually constituting interaction with late capitalism.

COLLECTIVE MINDS

The collective nature of networked, immaterial labour was exalted by the utopian statements of the 1990s cyberlibertarians. Kevin Kelly's popular thesis in *Out of Control*, for example, suggested that the Internet is a collective 'hive mind'. According to Kelly, the Internet is another manifestation of a principle of self-organization that is widespread throughout technical, natural and social systems. The Internet is the material evidence of the existence of the self-organizing, infinitely productive activities of connected human minds.[31] From a different perspective, Pierre Levy drew on cognitive anthropology and poststructuralist philosophy to argue that computers and computer networks enable the emergence of a 'collective intelligence'. Levy, who is inspired by early computer pioneers such as Douglas Engelbart, argues for a new humanism 'that incorporates and enlarges the scope of self-knowledge and collective thought'.[32] According to Levy, we are passing from a Cartesian model of thought based upon the singular idea of *cogito* (I think) to a collective or plural *cogitamus* (we think):

> What is collective intelligence? It is a form of *universally distributed intelligence,* constantly enhanced, coordinated in real time, and resulting in the effective mobilization of skills ... The basis and goal of collective intelligence is the mutual recognition and enrichment of individuals rather than the cult of fetishized or hypostatized communities.[33]

Like Kelly, Levy frames his argument within the common rhetoric of competition and flexibility which dominates the hegemonic discourse around digitalization: 'The more we are able to form intelligent communities, as open-minded, cognitive subjects capable of initiative, imagination, and rapid response, the more we will be able to ensure our success in a highly competitive environment.'[34] In Levy's view, the digital economy highlights the impossibility of absorbing intelligence within the process of automation: unlike the first wave of cybernetics, which displaced workers from the factory, computer networks highlight the unique value of human intelligence as the true creator of value in a knowledge economy. In his opinion, since the economy is increasingly reliant on the production of creative subjectivities, this production is highly likely to engender a new humanism, a new centrality of man's [sic] creative potentials.

Especially in Kelly's case, it has been easy to dismiss the notion of a 'hive mind' and the self-organizing Internet-as-free market as 'Internet gold rush' rhetoric, promptly demolished by more or less unexpected events of 2001 (dot-com crash, resurgence of international terrorism and imperialism). It was difficult to avoid a feeling of irritation at such willing oblivion of the realities of working in the high-tech industries, from the poisoning world of the silicon chips factories to the electronic sweatshops of America Online, where technical work is downgraded and workers' obsolescence is high.[35] How can we hold on to the notion that cultural production and immaterial labor are collective on the Net (both inner and outer) after the belated Y2K explosion in 2001 and without subscribing to the idealistic and teleological spirit of the wired revolution?

We could start with a simple observation: the self-organizing, collective intelligence of cybercultural thought captured the existence of networked immaterial labour, but was weak in its analysis of the operations of capital overall (including the coexistence of different capitalist lobbies and their relation to insitutional governance). Capital, after all, is the unnatural environment within which the collective intelligence materializes. The collective dimension of networked intelligence needs to be understood historically, as part of a specific momentum of capitalist development. The Italian writers who are identified with the post-Gramscian Marxism of Autonomia Operaia have consistently engaged with this relationship by focusing on the mutation undergone by labour in the aftermath of the factory. The notion of a self-organizing 'collective intelligence' looks uncannily like one of their central concepts, the 'general intellect', a notion that the autonomists 'extracted' out of the spirit, if not the actually wording, of Marx's *Grundrisse*. The 'collective intelligence' or 'hive mind' captures some of the spirit of the 'general intellect', but removes the autonomists' critical theorization of its relation to capital.

In the autonomists' favorite text, the *Grundrisse,* and especially in the 'Fragment on Machines', Marx argues (as summarized by Paolo Virno) that

knowledge – scientific knowledge in the first place, but not exclusively – tends to become precisely by virtue of its autonomy from production, nothing less than the principal productive force, thus relegating repetitive and compartmentalized labor to a residual position. Here one is dealing with knowledge ... which has become incarnate ... in the automatic system of machines.[36]

In the vivid pages of the 'Fragment', the 'other' Marx of the *Grundrisse* (adopted by the social movements of the 1960s and 1970s against the more orthodox endorsement of *Capital*) describes the system of industrial machines as a horrific monster of metal and flesh:

The production process has ceased to be a labour process in the sense of a process dominated by labour as its governing unity. Labour appears, rather, merely as a conscious organ, scattered among the individual living workers at numerous points of the mechanical system; subsumed under the total process of the machinery itself, as itself only a link of the system, whose unity exists not in the living workers, but rather in the living (active) machinery, which confronts his individual, insignificant doings as a mighty organism.[37]

The Italian autonomists extracted from these pages the notion of the 'general intellect' as 'the ensemble of knowledge ... which constitute the epicenter of social production'.[38] Unlike Marx's original formulation, however, the autonomists eschewed the modernist imagery of the general intellect as a hellish machine. They claimed that Marx completely identified the general intellect (or knowledge as the principal productive force) with fixed capital (the machine) and thus neglected to account for the fact that the general intellect cannot exist independently of the concrete subjects who mediate the articulation of the machines with each other. The general intellect is an articulation of fixed capital (machines) *and* living labour (the workers). If we see the Internet, and computer networks in general, as the latest machines – the latest manifestation of fixed capital – then it won't be difficult to imagine the general intellect as being alive and well today.

However the autonomists did not stop at describing the general intellect as an assemblage of humans and machines at the heart of postindustrial production. If this were the case, the Marxian monster of metal and flesh would just be updated to that of a world-spanning network, where computers use human beings as a way to allow the system of machinery (and therefore capitalist production) to function. The visual power of the Marxian description is updated by the cyberpunk snapshots of the immobile bodies of the hackers, electrodes like umbilical cords connecting them to the matrix, appendixes to a living, all-powerful cyberspace. Beyond the special-effects bonanza, the box-office success of *The Matrix* series validates the popularity of the paranoid interpretation of this mutation.

To the humanism implicit in this description, the autonomists have opposed the notion of a 'mass intellectuality', living labour in its function as the determining articulation of the general intellect. Mass intellectuality – as an ensemble, as a social body – 'is the repository of the indivisible knowledges of living subjects and of their linguistic cooperation ... an important part of knowledge cannot be deposited in machines, but ... it must come into being as the direct interaction of the labor force'.[39] As Virno emphasizes, mass intellectuality is not about the various roles of the knowledge workers, but is a '*quality* and a distinctive sign of the *whole* social labor force in the post-Fordist era'.[40]

The pervasiveness of the collective intelligence within both the managerial literature and Marxist theory could be seen as the result of a common intuition about the quality of labour in informated societies. Knowledge labour is inherently *collective*, it is always the result of a collective and social production of knowledge.[41] Capital's problem is how to extract as much value as possible (in the autonomists' jargon, to 'valorize') out of this abundant, and yet slightly untractable terrain.

Collective knowledge work, then, is not about those who work in the knowledge industry. But it is also not about employment. The mass layoffs in the dot-com sector have not stopped Internet content from growing or its technologies from mutating. The acknowledgement of the collective aspect of labour implies a rejection of the equivalence between labour and employment, which was already stated by Marx and further emphasized by feminism and the post-Gramscian autonomy.[42] Labour is not equivalent to waged labour. Such an understanding might help us to reject some of the hideous rhetoric of unemployment which turns the unemployed person into the object of much patronizing, pushing and nudging from national governments in industrialized countries (accept any available work or else ...) Often the unemployed are such only in name, in reality being the life-blood of the difficult economy of 'under the table', badly paid work, some of which also goes into the new media industry.[43] To emphasize how labour is not equivalent to employment also means to acknowledge how important free affective and cultural labour is to the media industry, old and new.

EPHEMERAL COMMODITIES AND FREE LABOUR

There is a continuity, and a break, between older media and new media in terms of their relationship to cultural and affective labour. The continuity seems to lie in their common reliance on their public/ users as productive subjects. The difference lies both in the mode of production and in the ways in which power/knowledge works in the two types. In spite of different national histories (some of which stress public service more than others), the television industry, for example, is relatively conservative: writers, producers, performers, managers, and technicians have definite roles within an industry still run by a few established players. The historical legacy of television as a technology for the construction of national identities also means that television is somehow always held more publicly accountable than the news media.

This does not mean that the old media do not draw on free labour; on the contrary. Television and the print media, for example, make abundant use of the free labour of their audiences/readers, but they also tend to structure the latter's contribution much more strictly, in terms of both economic organization and moralistic judgement. The price to pay for all those real-life TV experiences is usually a heavy dose of moralistic scaremongering: criminals are running amok on the streets and must be stopped by tough police action; wild teenagers lack self-esteem and need tough love; and selfish and two-faced reality TV contestants will eventually get their come-uppance. If this does not happen on the Internet, why is it then that the Internet is not the happy island of decentred, dispersed and pleasurable cultural production that its apologists claimed it to be?

The most obvious answer to such questions came spontaneously to the early Internet users, who blamed it on the commercialization of the Internet. E-commerce and progressive privatization were blamed for disrupting the free economy of the Internet, an economy of exchange which Richard Barbrook described as 'gift economy'.[44] Indeed, the Internet might have been a different place from what it is now. However it is almost unthinkable that capitalism could have stayed forever outside of the network, a mode of communication which is fundamental to its own organizational structure.

The outcome of the explicit interface between capital and the Internet is a digital economy which manifests all the signs of an acceleration of the capitalist logic of production. During its dot-com days, the digital economy was the fastest and most visible zone of production within late capitalist societies. New products, new trends and new cultures succeeded each other at anxiety-inducing pace. It was a business where you needed to replace your equipment/ knowledge, and possibly staff, every year or so.

At some point, the speed of the digital economy, its accelerated rhythms of obsolescence and its reliance on (mostly) 'immaterial' products seemed to fit in with the postmodern intuition about the changed status of the commodities whose essence was said to be meaning (or lack of it) rather than labour (as if the two could be separable).[45] The recurrent complaint that the Internet contributes to the disappearance of reality is then based *both* in humanistic concerns about 'real life' *and* in the postmodern nihilism of the recombinant commodity.[46] Hyperreality confirms the humanist nightmare of a society without humanity, the culmination of a progressive taking over of the realm of representation. Commodities on the Net are not material and are excessive (there is too much information, too many web sites, too much spam, too many mailing lists, too much clutter and noise) with relation to the limits of 'real' social needs.

It is possible, however, that the disappearance of the commodity is not a material disappearance, but its visible subordination to the quality of labour behind it. In this sense the commodity does not disappear as such; it rather becomes increasingly ephemeral, its duration becomes compressed, it becomes more of a process than a finished product. The role of continuous, creative, innovative labour as the ground of market value is crucial to the digital economy. The process of valorization (the production of monetary value) happens by foregrounding the quality of the labour which literally animates the commodity.

The digital economy, then, challenged the postmodern assumption that labour disappears while the commodity takes on and dissolves all meaning. In particular, the Internet foregrounds the extraction of value out of continuous, updateable work and is extremely labour-intensive. It is not enough to produce a good web site; you need to update it continuously to maintain interest in it and fight off obsolescence. Furthermore, you need updateable equipment (the general intellect is always an assemblage of humans and their machines), which in its turn is propelled by the intense collective labour of programmers, designers and workers. It is as if the acceleration of production has increased to the point where commodities, literally, turn into translucent objects. Commodities do not so much disappear as become more transparent, showing throughout their reliance on the labour which produces and sustains them. It is the labour of the designers and programmers that shows through a successful web site and it is the spectacle of that labour changing its product that keeps the users coming back. The commodity, then, is only as good as the labour that goes into it.

As a consequence, the sustainability of the Internet as a medium depends on massive amounts of labour (which is not equivalent to employment, as we have said), only some of which was hyper-compensated by the capricious logic of venture capitalism. Of the incredible amount of labour which sustains the Internet as a whole (from mailing list traffic to web sites to infrastructural questions), we can guess that a substantial amount of it is still 'free labour'.

Free labour, however, is not necessarily exploited labour. Within the early virtual communities, we are told, labour was really free: the labour of building a community was not compensated by great financial rewards (it was therefore 'free', unpaid), but it was also willingly conceded in exchange for the pleasures of communication and exchange (it was therefore 'free', pleasurable, not-imposed). In answer to members' requests, information was quickly posted and shared with a lack of mediation which the early netizens did not fail to appreciate. Howard Rheingold's book, somehow unfairly accused of middle-class complacency, is the most well-known account of the good old times of the old Internet, before the net-tourist overcame the net-pioneer.[47]

The free labour which sustains the Internet is acknowledged within many different sections of the digital literature. In spite of the volatile nature of the Internet economy (which yesterday was about community and portals, today is about P2P and wireless connections, and tomorrow, who knows … ?). the notion of users' labour maintains an ideological and material centrality which runs consistently throughout the turbulent succession of Internet fads. Commentators who would normally disagree, such as Howard Rheingold and Richard Hudson, concur on one thing; the best way to keep your site visible and thriving on the Web is to turn it into a space which is not only accessed, but somehow built by its users.[48] Users keep a site alive through their labour, the cumulative hours of accessing the site (thus generating advertising), writing messages, participating in conversations and sometimes making the jump to collaborators. Out of the 15,000 volunteers which keep AOL running, only a handful turned against it, the others stayed on. Such a feature seems endemic to the Internet in ways which can be worked on by commercialization, but not substantially altered. The 'open-source' movement, which relies on the free labour of Internet tinkers, is further evidence of this structural trend within the digital economy.

It is an interesting feature of the Internet debate (and evidence, somehow, of its masculine bias) that users' labour has attracted more attention in the case of the open-source movement than in that of mailing lists and websites. This betrays the persistence of an attachment to masculine understandings of labour within the digital economy: writing an operating system is still more worthy of attention than just chatting for free for AOL. This in spite of the fact that in 1996, at the peak of the volunteer moment, over 30,000 'community leaders' were helping AOL to generate at least $7 million a month.[49] Still, the open-source movement has drawn much more positive attention than the more diffuse user-labour described above. It is worth exploring because of the debates which it has provoked and its relation to the digital economy at large.

The open-source movement is a variation of the old tradition of shareware and freeware software, which substantially contributed to the technical development of the Internet. Freeware software is freely distributed and does not even request a payment from its users. Shareware software is distributed freely, but incurs a 'moral' obligation for the user to forward a small sum to the producer in order to sustain the shareware movement as an alternative economic model to the copyrighted software of giants such as Microsoft. 'Open source' 'refers to a model of software development in which the underlying code of a program – the source code a.k.a. the 'crown jewels' – is by definition made freely available to the general public for modification, alteration, and endless redistribution'.[50]

Far from being an idealistic, minoritarian practice, the open-source movement has attracted much media and financial attention. In 1999, Apache, an open-source web server, was the 'Web-server program of choice for more than half of all publicly accessible Web servers'[51] and has since then expanded to the point where Bavaria in Germany and the whole of China have recently announced a switchover to it. Open-source conventions are anxiously attended by venture capitalists, informed by the digerati that open source is a necessity 'because you must go open-source to get access to the benefits of the open-source development community – the near-instantaneous bug-fixes, the distributed intellectual resources of the Net, the increasingly large open-source code base'.[52] Open-source companies such as Cygnus convinced the market that you do not need to be proprietary about source code to make a profit: the code might be free, but technical support, packaging, installation software, regular upgrades, office applications and hardware are not.

In 1998, when Netscape went open source and invited the computer tinkers and hobbyists to look at the code of its new browser, fix the bugs, improve the package and redistribute it, specialized mailing lists exchanged opinions about the implications.[53] Netscape's move rekindled the debate about the peculiar nature of the digital economy. Was it to be read as being in the tradition of the Internet 'gift economy'? Or was digital capital hijacking the open-source movement exactly against that tradition? Richard Barbrook saluted Netscape's move as a sign of the power intrinsic in the architecture of the medium.[54] Others such as John Horvarth did not share such optimism. The 'free stuff' offered around the Net, he argued,

> is either a product that gets you hooked on to another one or makes you just consume more time on the net. After all, the goal of the access people and telecoms is to have users spend as much time on the net as possible, regardless of what they are doing. The objective is to have you consume bandwidth.[55]

Far from proving the persistence of the Internet gift economy, Horvarth claimed, Netscape's move is a direct threat to those independent producers for whom shareware and freeware have been a way of surviving exactly those 'big boys' that Netscape represents:

> Freeware and shareware are the means by which small producers, many of them individuals, were able to offset somewhat the bulldozing effects of the big boys. And now the bulldozers are headed straight for this arena. As for Netscrape [sic], such a move makes good business sense and spells trouble for workers in the field of software development. The company had a poor last quarter in 1997 and was already hinting at job cuts. Well, what better way to shed staff by having your product taken further by the freeware people, having code-dabbling hobbyists fix and further develop your product? The question for Netscrape [sic] now is how to tame the freeware beast so that profits are secured.[56]

Although it is tempting to stake the evidence of crashes and layoffs against the optimism of Barbrook's gift economy, there might be more productive ways of looking at the increasingly tight relationship between an 'idealistic' movement such as open source and the venture mania for open-source companies.[57] Rather than representing a moment of incorporation of a previously authentic moment, the open-source question demonstrates the overreliance of the digital economy as such on free labour, free both in the sense of 'not financially rewarded' and of 'willingly given'. This includes AOL community leaders, the open-source programmers, the amateur web designers, mailing list editors and the netslaves who for a while were willing to 'work for cappucinos' just for the excitement and the dubious promises of digital work.[58]

Such a reliance, almost a dependency, is part of larger mechanisms of capitalist extraction of value which are fundamental to late capitalism as a whole. That is, such processes are not created outside capital and then reappropriated by capital, but are the results of a complex history where the relation between labour and capital is mutually constitutive, entangled and crucially forged during the crisis of Fordism. Free labour is a desire of labour immanent to late capitalism, and late capitalism is the field which both sustains free labour *and* exhausts it. It exhausts it by undermining the means through which that labour can sustain itself: from the burn-out syndromes of Internet start-ups to under-compensation and exploitation in the cultural economy at large. Late capitalism does not appropriate anything: it nurtures, exploits and exhausts its labour force and its cultural and affective production. In this sense, it is technically impossible to separate neatly the digital economy of the Net from the larger network economy of late capitalism. Especially since 1994, the Internet has always and simultaneously been a gift economy *and* an advanced capitalist economy. The mistake of the neoliberalists (as exemplified by the *Wired* group), was to mistake this coexistence for a benign, unproblematic equivalence.

As we stated before, these processes are far from being confined to the most self-conscious labourers of the digital economy. They are part of a diffuse cultural economy which operates throughout the Internet and beyond. The passage from the pioneeristic days of the Internet to its 'venture' and 'recession' days does not seem to have affected these mechanisms, only intensified them. Nowhere is this more evident that on the World Wide Web.

THE NET AND THE SET

In the winter of 1999, in what sounded like another of its resounding, short-lived claims, *Wired* magazine announced that after just five years the old Web was dead:

> The Old Web was a place where the unemployed, the dreamy, and the iconoclastic went to reinvent themselves ... The New Web isn't

about dabbling in what you don't know and failing – it's about preparing seriously for the day when television and Web content are delivered over the same digital networks.[59]

The new Web was made of the big players, but also of new ways to make the audience work. In the new Web, after the pioneering days, television and the web converge in the one thing they have in common: their reliance on their audiences/users as providers of the cultural labour which goes under the label of 'real life stories'. Gerry Laybourne, executive of the web-based media company *Oxygen,* thought of a hypothetical show called *What Are They Thinking?* a reality-based sketch comedy show based on stories posted on the Web, because 'funny things happen in our lives everyday'.[60] As Bayers also adds, '[u]ntil it's produced, the line separating that concept from more puerile fare dismissed by Gerry, like *America's Funniest*, is hard to see'.[61]

The difference between the puerile fare of *America's Funniest* and user-produced content does not seem to lie in the more serious nature of the new Web as compared to the vilified output of 'people shows' and 'reality television'. From an abstract point of view there is no difference between the ways in which people shows rely on the inventiveness of their audiences and the web sites rely on users' input. People shows rely on the activity (even amidst the most shocking sleaze) of their audience and willing participants to a much larger extent than any other television programmes. In a sense, they manage the impossible; they create monetary value out of the most reluctant members of the postmodern cultural economy: those who do not produce marketable style, who are not qualified enough to enter the fast world of the knowledge economy, are converted into monetary value through their capacity to *affectively* perform their misery.

When compared to the cultural and affective production on the Internet, people shows and reality TV also seem to embody a different logic of relation between capitalism (the media conglomerates which produce and distribute such shows) and its labour force – the beguiled, dysfunctional citizens of the underdeveloped North. Within people shows and reality TV, the valorization of the audience as labour and spectacle always happens somehow within a power/ knowledge nexus which does not allow the *immediate* valorization of the talk show participants: you cannot just put a Jerry Springer guest on TV on her own to tell her story with no mediation (indeed that would look too much like the discredited access slots of public service broadcasting). There is no real 24/7 access to reality TV, but increasing/decreasing levels of selective editing (according to the different modalities of a communication spectrum that goes from terrestrial to digital TV and the Internet). In the case of talk shows, various levels of knowledge intervene between the guest and the apparatus of valorization, which normalize the dysfunctional subjects through a moral or therapeutic discourse and a more traditional institutional organization of production. So after the performance, the guest must be advised, patronized, questioned and often bullied by the audience and the host, all in the name of a perfunctory, normalizing morality. In reality television, psychologists and other experts are also brought in to provide an authoritative perspective through which what is often a sheer voyeuristic experience may be seen as a 'social experiment'.

TV shows also belong to a different economy of scale: although there are more and more of them, they are still relatively few when compared to the millions of pages on the Web. It is as if the centralized organization of the traditional media does not let them turn people's productions into pure monetary value. TV shows must have morals, even if those morals are shattered by the overflowing performances of their subjects.

Within the Internet, however, this process of channelling and adjudicating (responsibilities, duties and rights) is dispersed to the point where practically anything is tolerated (sadomasochism, bestiality, fetishism and plain nerdism are not targeted, at least within the Internet, as sites which need to be disciplined or explained away). The qualitative difference between people shows and a successful web site, then, does not lie in the latter's democratic tendency as opposed to the former's exploitative nature. It lies in the operation, within people shows, of majoritarian discursive mechanisms of territoralization, the application of a morality that the 'excessive' abundance of material on the Internet renders redundant and, even more, irrelevant. The digital economy cares only tangentially about morality. What it really cares about is an abundance of production, an immediate interface with cultural and technical labour whose result is a diffuse, non-dialectical antagonism and a crisis in the capitalist modes of valorization of labour as such.

As we shall see in the next chapter, it would be a mistake to think of such trends as constituting an automatic process of liberation from the tyranny of capitalist exploitation. On the contrary, as we have also suggested here, this open and distributed mode of production is already the field of experimentation of new strategies of organization that starts from the open potentiality of the many in order to develop new sets of constraints able to modulate appropriately the relation between value and surplus value – or, as we will refer to them, the entanglement of emergence and control.

4
Soft Control

BIOLOGICAL COMPUTING

Writing in 1934, a few years before the first digital computers were assembled in the United States, technology historian Lewis Mumford called for an end to the numbing power of the industrial technological milieu and for it to be replaced by a new technological age – free from the dominance of the mechanical rationality of the clock and the deadening sensorial influence of materials such as iron and coal. Mumford thought that the future of technological development lay in a return to the organic, a return that he also significantly saw at the heart of research into modern mass media:[1] the study of the ear, throat and tongue, he remarked, had been fundamental to the development of the phonograph; and research on motion in horses, oxen, bulls, greyhounds, deer, and birds provided the basis for the scientific study of the relationship between images and movements that produced the motion picture. Mumford suggested that technological innovation was not intrinsically tied to the domination of nature, as the Baconian model implies, but also entailed a more challenging relationship with the *artficiality* of the natural world. Human technicity does not so much construct increasingly elaborate extensions of man, but rather intensifies at specific points its engagement with different levels of the organization of nature. Such levels are abstracted and redeployed within the complex social machines within which human and technical segments arrange themselves. The nature that emerges out of this interaction is itself not only complex, but also 'artificial', that is inventive and productive. Far from being synonymous with an eternal and immutable essence, the natural world comes across as multiple and complex, endowed with its own ingenious, adaptive and inhuman creativity.[2] And machines, as George Canguilhem and Felix Guattari would put it later, can be more than mere mechanisms.

Mumford's call for an organic complication of the mechanical would not sound out of place in an age where communication networks are often described as self-organizing, evolutionary and

98

bottom-up. Above all, the explosion of the Internet phenomenon has induced a rush to compare and contrast its workings with those of other systems endowed with a similar logic (from swarms to markets). Drawing on the insights of population biology, apologists for free markets and bottom-up organization have pointed out the ubiquity of the latter in the realm of the 'made and the born'.[3] 'New Economy' endorsers claimed to be inspired by the ubiquity of evolutionary processes and their capacity not only to sort out the fit from the unfit, but also actively to produce the variety of life as such. This use of evolutionary theory pointed to an artificial nature – that is a nature that was made and unmade by specific and complex techniques that it produced immanently and without a predefined purpose or aim.

Inspired by the work of formidable computing pioneers such as John von Neumann and Stanislav Ulam, the field of biological computing that is the focus of this chapter has engaged with the technicity of nature as expressed in evolutionary processes and has thus been criticized as a sustained and misleading attempt to naturalize technical and social relations – giving support to the notion of a self-organizing Internet intrinsically given over to the beneficial action of free-market forces. Biological computing, in fact, is centrally concerned with understanding phenomena of bottom-up organization by simulating the conditions of their emergence in an artificial medium – the digital computer. The term refers to a cluster of subdisciplines within the computer sciences – such as artificial life (which aims to develop lifelike behaviour within computer simulations); mobotics (the engineering of mobile robots that are able to learn from their mistakes); and neural networks (a bottom-up approach to artificial intelligence that starts with simple networks of neurons rather than with top-down sets of instructions). What these subdisciplines share is a common reference to John von Neumann's work in the 1950s with cellular automata – a go-like game entailing an open chequerboard and a population of squares bound by local rules of interaction. Von Neumann's cellular automata have been demonstrated to be capable of universal computation (just like the universal Turing machine).

Since von Neumann's times, the field of biological computing has developed into a well-funded and profitable field of research with important applications in areas as different as animation and cancer research. It has absorbed insights from chaos theory, molecular biology, population thinking and, of course, evolutionary theory. Its field of interest can be described as the capacity of acentred and leaderless multitudes of simple elements, bound only by local rules, to produce *emergent phenomena* able to outperform the programmers' instructions. Biological computing explores the larger plane of abstract machines of bottom-up organization, of which the Internet appears as a specific instance and product. What makes such machines abstract is their lack of qualities: they are no more technical than they are natural, nor could they be described as biological rather than social. Their simulation involves the description of an abstract diagram that brings into relation almost indefinite entities, laws and capacities – acentred multitudes; local rules; global dynamics; capacity to engender emergence; relative unpredictability; refractoriness to control. What biological computing asks is: How do such systems come to be? What are they made of? What rules explain them? How can they be re-created and what kind of control modes are better suited to their immense potential and refractory tendencies?

If the network is a type of 'spatial diagram' for the age of global communication, the self-organizing, bottom-up machines of biological computation capture the network not simply as an abstract topological formation – but as a new type of *production machine*. In this sense, as we shall see, the processes studied and replicated by biological computation are more than just a techno-ideological expression of market fundamentalism. Biological computation implies an informational milieu where each point is directly connected to its immediate neighbours (on whom it acts and to whom it reacts); and is indirectly, but no less effectively, affected by the movements of the whole. A self-organizing system engendering emergent behaviour (that is, behaviour that has not been explicitly programmed or commanded) expresses a mode of production that is characterized by an *excess* of value – an excess that demands flexible strategies of valorization and control. In the next pages, then, we will explore that entanglement of the organic and the inorganic, the physical and the biological, and the natural and the technological, in order to catch a glimpse of the emergence of a kind of *abstract machine of soft control* – a diagram of power that takes as its operational field the productive capacities of the hyperconnected many. But first, we shall proceed to a preliminary outline of what the shift to biological computation implies and its relation to the larger epistemic field of contemporary scientific knowledge.

FROM ORGANISMS TO MULTITUDES

The biological turn in computing, with its interest in natural and artificial bottom-up organization, can be thought of as part of a larger techno-scientific reconceptualization of life – beyond the mechanical laws of classical science, but also beyond the organized forms of modern anatomy and biology. For artificial life theorists such as Charles Taylor and David Jefferson, all natural life can be understood in terms of the interactions of a large number of simple elements from levels below. The living organism is no longer mainly one single and complicated biochemical machine, but is now essentially the aggregate result of the interaction of a large *population* of relatively simple machines.[4] These populations of interacting simple machines are working at all levels of the biophysical organization of matter. They are active at the molecular level, the cellular level, the organism level, and the population–ecosystem level.[5] As a consequence, 'to animate machines, ... is not to "bring" life to *a* machine; rather it is to organize a population of machines in such a way that their interactive dynamics is "alive"'.[6] Mary Shelley's Frankenstein, therefore, started from the wrong premises. If you want to reproduce the complexity of life, you do not start with organs, stitch them all together and then shock them into life. You start more humbly and modestly, *at the bottom*, with a multitude of interactions in a liquid and open milieu.

The computational disintegration of the organism into a multitude of interacting, simple machines is also observable in current connectionist approaches to the mind, at the basis of recent artificial intelligence work that attempts to model the behaviour of the central nervous system (CNS). By studying the dynamics of neural cells in the CNS, recent work in artificial intelligence is hoping to reproduce some of the complex features of the mind, such as its capacity to recognize patterns and to hold an 'indefinite memory'. Very simplified models of neural nets, such as networks of fixed threshold neurons, 'have learned to distinguish a variety of complex patterns; faces, handwriting, spoken words, sonar signals and stock market fluctuations have all served as grist for such networks.'[7]

A bottom-up approach, as the expression indicates, implies that one does not start with the already formed and stratified organ, such as the brain, or with a faculty, the mind, but that one reconstructs the conditions that underlie and produce, as an after-effect, that organ or faculty. Modern science conceived of thinking as a capacity located in a specific part of the human body, which could be damaged and easily destroyed if the organ was attacked. Thus if by accident or experiment a part of the brain is destroyed, with it go some of our memories and capacity to grasp the world. Neural nets are inspired by connectionist approaches to cognition that reject an understanding of the mind in terms of the morphology of the brain (or imply the presence of a representational cognitive box, as Rodney Brooks has put it)[8]. Here the brain and the mind are dissolved into the dynamics of emergence, the outcome of a multitude of molecular, semi-ordered interactions between large populations of connected neurons.

While organisms haven't stopped being damaged by the destruction of individual organs, and the rational and perceptive capacities of individuals can still be dramatically affected by a physical blow to the head, such a conception of cognition is no longer occupying the centre stage of contemporary research into the artificiality of the mind. From the conception of the brain as a specialized organ that acts like a storage for memories and a coordinator for the whole body, connectionism moves on to outline the feature of a mind that is no longer located anywhere specific. As Gregory Bateson put it:

> [W]e may say that 'mind' is immanent in those circuits of the brain that are completely within the brain. Or that mind is immanent in circuits which are complete within the system brain *plus* body. Or finally, that mind is immanent in the larger system – man plus environment.[9]

In biological computing, the organism is sidestepped from above and from beneath: from above it dissolves into the collectivity of its connections (the mind plus its environment); and from beneath it is sidestepped by the parallel-processing features of the neurons in the brain and the central nervous system. Thus cognitive science becomes Bergsonian. Memories are not images that are stored somewhere in the brain, but emergent events assembled out of many discrete fragments in an act of partial reinvention. 'These pieces of half-thoughts have no fixed home; they abide throughout the brain … The act of perceiving and the act of remembering are the same. Both assemble an emergent whole from many distributed pieces.'[10]

In artificial life research, the attempt to breed artificial forms of life is explicitly related to the dynamic of populations, whose local interaction produces a lifelike effect. 'It is this bottom-up distributed, local determination of behavior that AL employs in its primary methodological approach to the generation of lifelike behavior.'[11] This can include the capacity of a robot to walk by letting its legs interact according to simple rules or the artificial evolution of software through genetic algorithms. Rather than being pre-programmed sequentially and inbuilt in hardware, these experiments aim to 'evolve' lifelike behaviour. The biological turn is thus unabashedly mechanistic and reductionist: all life is reduced to a simple set of local rules governing the behaviour of simple machines. But, it claims, its mechanicism is deeply different from the old one, 'based as it is on multiplicities of machines and on recent results in the field of nonlinear dynamics, chaos theory, and the formal theory of computation'.[12]

Biological computation is thus concerned with the power of the small. Small here should not be taken to indicate size and weight in the metrical sense. Smallness is not measured by rulers and scales, but it is exterior and relational: it is described by an overall relation to a large number of variables, with no ultimate determination or central control. What determines the ultimate lack of any distinction between the natural and the artificial is ultimately the indetermination of a multitude. An individual broker within a large and turbulent stock market is as small as a molecule within a turbulent fluid. What makes the components of an open system small is not their size but the fact that they are grasped in terms of their overall relation to a large number of interchangeable components that interact on each other by way of recursive feedback loops. These systems do not simply die or reproduce themselves by way of an autopoietic movement, but they are always becoming something else: 'They are forever dynamic and can be considered dead and of little interest when they come to thermodynamic equilibrium. It is really the dynamic properties of complexity, the motion pictures, not the snapshots, which characterize the systems in which we are interested.'[13]

All these processes are grasped in terms not only of their risks but also of their potential conceived from the perspective of the *replicability* of open and productive structures. Thus Silicon Valley in the San Francisco Bay Area has been similarly analysed as a kind of ecosystem for the development of 'disruptive technologies', 'whose growth and success can be attributed to the incessant formation of a multitude of specialized, diverse entities that feed off, support and interact with one another.'[14] Such concerns have preoccupied different governments keen to replicate the success of the Silicon Valley postindustrial ecosystem. If the latter was not planned in any

traditional sense, but emerged as a hotbed of technological innovations out of a multiplicity of different factors and connections, how
can one replicate the same process elsewhere? A combination of
the very small and the very large implies a shift in the organization
of productivity, but how should this be accomplished if there is no
formula that will fit all cases?

The matter is then not so much about cracking the secret of the
micro in its entirety, but understanding the initial conditions, that,
once got right, allow a certain kind of outcome to emerge *spontaneously*. 'Emergence must somehow be bound up in the selection of
the rules (mechanisms) that specify the model, be it game or physical
science.'[15] The outcome is not programmed step by step, but is,
rather, carefully prepared at the beginning and there is no guarantee
of success – as Manuel Castells and Peter Hall's study of failed attempts
at recreating the conditions for the emergence of milieus of innovation
has also shown.[16]

The most important feature of the systems studied and simulated
within biological computing is that they are not easily controllable
or predictable. A multitude of simple bodies in an open system is by
definition acentred and leaderless. There is no single control structure
that can be manipulated or attacked: the sheer multiplicity of
nonlinear interactions, feedback loops, and mutations make the
behaviour of such systems very hard to analyse, because it is
impossible to control them completely and unequivocally (even the
simple activity of observing them alters them). They cannot be
known completely because they cannot be studied by dissection:
once the connection and mutual affection with other elements is
removed, the individual element becomes passive and inert. In the
shift from the bug to the hive colony, from the individual to the
population, from the Internet user to a network culture, something
happens and this something, although somehow inherent in the
bug/individual, cannot be found in it by any of the traditional means
(it is both pre-individual and collective). You can observe and kill an
individual entity, anatomize it, and you still won't find out what it
is that will make it act in a certain way once it acts as an element
within a population open to flows. You can collect as much data as
you want about individual users, but this won't give you the dynamic
of the overall network.

This leads us to wonder what else is packed into the bee that we
haven't seen yet? Or what else is packed into the hive that has not

yet appeared because there haven't been enough honeybee hives in a row all at once? And for that matter, what is contained in a human that will not emerge until we are all interconnected by wires and politics?[17]

Knowing what it is that is packed into an individual but that is not reducible to it is a matter of some importance considering how inherently unstable such systems are. A multitude can always veer off somewhere unexpected under the spell of some strange attractor. On the other hand, while difficult to control, these systems are characterized by a potentially enormous productivity, what the literature on the subject describes as their dynamic capacity to support 'engaging events', while acting with a high degree of distributed 'autonomy and creativity'. This autonomy and creativity is produced by a process of recursive looping that generates divergent and transmittable variations at all points. Such systems, that is, are characterized by their tendency to escape from themselves, continually diverging; at the same time, such divergence does not generate complete differentiation because such mutations are spread by way of diagonal and transversal dynamics. Finally, there is no guarantee that such bottom-up dynamics will lead to emergent behaviour: systems can also come to a standstill or veer off catastrophically in unexpected directions.

A crucial problem for the simulation of the behaviour of such entities is that of reproducing the right speed, that is the right degree of boundedness, of a multitude. A bottom-up system, in fact, seems to appear almost spontaneously not so much as a result of a change in the composition of individual elements, but more in relation to how loosely such elements can interact with each other (it is a function of their overall *speed*). A multitude, for example, is quite foreign to sequentiality, whether it is the linear and closed sequentiality of the assembly line or the one-directional flow of broadcasting. When segments are connected together in a single line, they become immediately bound to each other and to the overall structure and hence geared towards reproduction rather than becoming. Similarly, a transversely-connected multitude is quite alien to the logic of mass societies, in as much as the solidity and boundedness of the mass tend towards the production of homeostasis, that is an increasing homogenization, while a multitude tends to engender, multiply and spread mutations. 'We should learn more about predicting and controlling critical stages in the process of emergence. This knowledge, in turn, should help us to understand better the processes that crown human intellectual undertakings: innovation and creation.'[18]

SEARCHING A PROBLEM SPACE

New Economy capitalism made much of the relationship between bottom-up organization and speed and focused on the importance of fluidity as a physical condition. At a certain level of speed, in a semi-ordered or *liquid phase,* large numbers are subject to a different kind of rules than solid and bound entities.

> It has long been appreciated by science that large numbers behave differently than small numbers. Mobs breed a requisite measure of complexity for emergent entities. The total number of possible interactions between two or more members accumulates exponentially as the number of members increases. At a high level of connectivity, and a high number of members, the dynamics of mobs takes hold. More *is* different.[19]

Moreness, then, as Kevin Kelly put it, is explicitly linked to the need for a different immanent logic of organization that demands new strategies of control to take advantage of its potentially infinite productivity while controlling its catastrophic potential. So it should not surprise us how much biological computing owes to the mechanics of fluids.

In his eulogy of bottom-up organization written at the height of the 'free market' digital wave, Kevin Kelly quoted the writings of C. Lloyd Morgan, who in his 1923 book *Emergent Evolution* defined emergent phenomena as 'a different variety of causation': '[t]he emergent step, though it may seem more or less saltatory [a leap], is best regarded as a qualitative change of direction, or critical turning-point, in the course of events.'[20] In this sense, the biological turn entails a rediscovery, that of the ancient *clinamen* (or swerve) – the explanation given by the pre-Socratic philosopher Epicurus for the existence of a principle of indeterminacy in the form of chance in atomic theory.[21] This swerve or clinamen, a principle of chance and indetermination, is identified by Ilya Prigogine and Isabelle Stengers as a crucial intuition into the features of 'far-from-equilibrium systems, systems that is that are very sensitive to fluctuations'.[22] Michel Serres associates the clinamen with the ancient Lucretian notions of *turbo* and *turba.*

The minimal angle of turbulence produces the first spirals here and there. It is literally revolution or it is the first evolution toward something else other than the same. Turbulence perturbs the chain, troubling the flow of the identical as Venus had troubled Mars.[23]

For Michel Serres, the sciences of the clinamen take as their central concern fluctuations, deviations, and instability. In the biological turn such features are not discarded or pushed outside the perimeter of legitimate scientific investigation, as was the case, as Prigogine and Stengers argued, with classical science from Aristotle to Clausius. The acknowledgement of an original difference/clinamen/deviation (a microdeterritorialization or line of flight) is taken as the object of study in order to develop a better knowledge of, and implicit control over, the action of randomness and chance in populations at the point where they have lost all social qualities and qualifications. Within financial and investment banking, for example, in the randomness and chance inherent in markets characterized by high fluidity of currency and investment patterns, such uncertainty is considered a source not only of potentially immense profitability but also of dreaded, abrupt changes – the kind of changes that can depress stock markets for years or trigger new types of global wars. For management theory, autonomy in the workplace is a similarly volatile compound: it represents a highly productive source of value but can also dangerously veer in unprofitable directions. Within bureaucratic organizations such as governments, banks, and corporations, flows are looked at with mixed feelings, from glee and greed to suspicion.

The biological turn in computing gives such mixed feelings a solid basis in scientific knowledge and technical experimentation, where fluid states are considered essential conditions for emergence. The synthesis of emergent phenomena out of a fluid and hence uncertain organization is described as a search for a particular 'phase space', which is characterized by a specific level of speed:

> ... there was a certain area where information changed but not so rapidly that it lost all connection to where it had just been previously. This was akin to a liquid state. ... it was the liquid regime that supported the most engaging events, those that would support the kind of complexity that was the mark of living systems.[24]

The question is how to maintain the productivity of a *fluid* space, dynamically perched between the unproductive extremes of solidity and gaseous chaos. Or as Tim Berners-Lee put it, '[w]e certainly need a structure that will avoid those two catastrophes: the global uniform McDonald's monoculture, and the isolated Heaven's Gate cults that understand only themselves.'[25] It is a matter then of finding the right speed that facilitates activity.

> To use somewhat anthropomorphic language: in equilibrium matter is 'blind', but in far-from-equilibrium conditions it begins to be able to perceive, to take into 'account' in its way of functioning, differences in the external world (such as weak gravitational or electrical fields).[26]

A fluid state is thus defined as a relation of speed determining the level of connection loosely binding a multitude of simple bodies or machines. A fluid space is characterized by a loose relation between molecules or components which allows them the capacity to deviate and spontaneously produce turbulent phenomena. A space of flows engenders emergent phenomena but does not guarantee that they will always be of use or even advantage to the experimenter or the planner, because they are open to sudden transformations or catastrophes. Since planning is confined to the initial conditions, preferred outcomes can only be hoped for rather than counted on. Emergent output needs to be carefully collected and valorized at the end of the process with a very fine-toothed comb; it must be *modulated* with a minimum amount of force. It cannot be analysed, but only *synthesized,* by experimenting with the set of *constraints* that facilitate it. This is a control of a specific type, it is a *soft control.* It is not soft because it is less harsh (often it has nothing gentle about it) but because it is an experiment in the control of systems that respond violently and often suicidally to rigid control.

GLOBAL COMPUTATION

Biological computing applies the algebraic logic of Boolean functions to local interactions among artificial populations of code. In this, biological computing follows population thinking – a perspective on life that brings together evolutionism and genetics.

> In a nutshell what characterizes this style may be phrased as 'never think in terms of Adam and Eve but always in terms of larger reproductive communities'. More technically, the idea is that

despite the fact that at any one time an evolved form is realized in individual organisms, the population not the individual is the matrix for the production of form.[27]

Population thinking considers a given form, such as an animal, as the statistical result of a larger process of diffusion of genetic material at different rates and different times. Population thinking has produced a great awareness of transversal genetic lines cutting across biological forms, their variations and the coevolutionary processes that have produced the variety of populations and complex organisms on earth. Although some populations can become isolated by geological accidents (as with the Moa in New Zealand, for example), generally speaking populations operate as open systems. The differential rates of diffusion of genetic material across and within populations can be computed over time and such computation highlights the fluctuations and leaps that characterize the evolution of life.[28] For Stuart Kauffmann, the meeting between population biology, Darwinism and genetics is crucial to contemporary understandings of life. Contemporary evolutionary biology has learned to connect the historical variation of species and populations in terms of the diffusion of genes and genetic variations under the aegis of natural selection. The link between evolutionary biology and computation dates back to John von Neumann's work in the aftermath of World War II with a computational experiment called 'cellular automata': (or CAs) – 'a relatively new field that appeared in the midst of the intellectual dust that accompanied the development of the first digital computers'.[29] This interest was a recurring concern of information theory and computer science (Claude E. Shannon's mentor, Vannevar Bush, also encouraged him to write his MA thesis on the relationship between information and genetics). Von Neumann's CAs, however, are the most common point of reference for biological computation. They were devised as an alternative approach to computation that was originally developed as a means to formalize the characteristics of life – in tune with the formalist spirit that we know informed the emergence of the Turing machine. CAs can also be seen as a complex kind of game, and it is as a game, such as John Conway's game of life, that CAs are probably best known outside computational circles.

According to John Holland, a leading researcher in artificial life, the original impulse for the construction of cellular automata came from Stanislav Ulam, who was interested in 'model physics', that is mathematical models of the physical universe that obeyed the two main laws of physics: they had to have a geometry and a set of locally defined laws that held at every point of the geometry. In a series of lectures entitled 'General and Logical Theory of Automata', von Neumann showed how such model physics could be used to replicate one of the key formal features of life, that is, *self-reproduction*. He thus embarked on building a formal model that could be shown as capable of making copies of itself by simply following a set of mechanical and local rules. His models of self-reproducing automata, or CAs, were shown to correspond to the mechanisms driving the replication of genetic material in the cell and are also considered today as serious alternatives to Alan Turing's universal computer. Variations of von Neumann's CAs (such as quantum cellular automata) are also researched in terms of their potential to take computing power beyond the limits of current microchip manufacturing technology. Cellular automata machines (such as Tom Toffoli and Norman Margolus's dedicated CA computer CAM-8) have been shown to be able to simulate dynamical systems that are beyond the reach of conventional computers and even supercomputers, such as fluid mechanics. 'The particles in fluids can be represented in such detail that Toffoli now considers that he is not working with a computational system but instead he says he is manipulating "programmable matter"'.[30]

The key idea of CAs is that there are formal structures that are able to perform *global computation* through a system of *local rules* that simply dictate the relationship of each cell/particle/node with its neighbours. In a cellular automata system, every cell reacts exclusively to the state of its neighbours and it is on this basis that it changes. The cumulative result of these changes has been shown to be capable of universal computation, with some classes of cellular automata able to model the behaviour of chaotic and open systems. CAs can be played like a game, in as much as they involve the invention of rules and their application to a population of cells.

In spite of their random appearance, cellular automata have been shown as capable of computing. This is no mean feat, since to use cellular automata to solve an equation requires asking hundreds of thousand of components to produce a reliable result by reacting individually but in a strictly determined manner to the behaviour of their neighbours. And yet computer simulations of CA systems have proved that you can solve equations in this way, even though it involves a process of trying, testing and running hundreds of simulations until one hits on the solution. A classic example of a cellular automata system able to perform very complex calculations is the nervous system – with its millions of simultaneous local interactions producing conscious perception by way of emergence.[31] CAs have also been shown to be able to successfully model complex phenomena ranging from the role of neutral and selective mutations in cancer to the dynamics of neural nets; from call-routing using adaptive pricing to the emergence of social morals and computer assisted design in architecture.

Biological computing envisages an abstract computational diagram able to simulate (and hence capture) the productive capacities of multitudes of discrete and interacting elements. The most productive challenge of CA systems to the sequential computer lies in the fact that they do not start with the easily controllable linearity of a tape, but with the multiplicity of a population. What produces the computation is not a sequence of instructions carried out by an individual probe head, but a multitude of simultaneous interactions performed by a potentially infinite population. A CA system, in fact, can be imagined as an open chequerboard space divided into a potentially infinite number of cells/nodes each one of which can be in a number of states (von Neumann devised a very complex CA with 29 states, but the game of life has only two: dead or alive). In a two-dimensional CA, each node is linked to eight neighbouring nodes. The single node will change its state by following a rule table that dictates what it should do in relation to each specific configuration of the other eight cells. Thus, if the eight neighbouring cells are blue, for example, the central cell would obey an instruction that says that if they are all blue, it should turn yellow. Its turning yellow would in turn affect the states of neighbouring cells, and so on. All changes of phase happen simultaneously according to discrete time steps. CA researchers have shown that simply by playing around with the initial configurations and the rule table, one can get such populations of cells to replicate any other machine – exactly like a universal Turing machine, but using a different logic that involves the collective and decentralized work of populations in synchronized, local and nonlinear relations. Different CA systems differ in terms of the number of dimensions considered (there are one-dimensional and two-dimensional CAs although they could theoretically have any number of dimensions); and the states which the cells can be in (they range between the dead/alive state of the game of life to von

Neumann's 29 states). More importantly, CA systems can differ in terms of the rule tables that dictate the changes of state of each node (what Christopher Langton has called the 'genotype' of the CA). Each rule table will produce different configurations depending on the initial state of the cells (in ALife jargon, the name for these different configurations engendered by identical rule tables is 'phenotypes'). This simple model constitutes a type of computation that is locally connected but spatially extended and capable of global computation. There is no central control determining what each cell should do according to a general blueprint or master plan. Each cell is subject to the same table of rules according to which it changes state at every time step together with all its neighbours. All the interactions take place at the local level, depending simply on the relationship between each cell and its neighbours. And yet this decentralized system of rules has been shown as capable of producing a high-level computation that cannot be explained through the action of individual cells. CAs underplay the importance of individual in favour of collective dynamics. This collective dynamics, however, is not related back to the action of a central agency in charge of regulating the fluctuations, but is capable of spontaneous self-regulation. CAs form dynamic milieus, space–time blocks, that have no real territorial qualities but do have rich topographies and challenging dynamics.

Unlike Turing machines, which George Caffentzis has likened to a kind of Taylorism of intellectual work, CA machines cannot really be programmed in the usual sense.[32] It is impossible, that is, to determine a priori the sequence of configurations that running a CA experiment will produce, once a set of rules and an initial configuration are given. There is no prediction involved, but a strategy of proliferation and selection. If one runs a CA genotype long enough, something good may come out of it. If it doesn't, however, there is no point in trying to fix it. Other genotypes, involving different sets of rules, will be found that are more successful in completing the task. CAs systems can be classified only a posteriori, that is after they have been tried out.

Researchers such as Stephen Wolfram and Christopher Langton have tried to produce some kind of classification of such distributed computational systems. Wolfram was the first to accomplish an empirical classification of CA dynamical systems by cataloguing 100 runs of the game of life. As a result of his survey, he found that most CAs fit within four classes. Class I CAs were those programs that for some reasons ended up running out of computational capabilities very quickly by reaching a limit or end point after which no computation was possible. Class II CAs, on the other hand, are characterized by what chaos theorists describe as 'limit cycles': they produce self-replicating structures (such as gliders) that spread across the computational space by self-replication. Class III and IV CAs, however, express a qualitative jump in complexity with relation to the other two. Class III CAs produce fractal structures, that is forms that do not simply repeat themselves, like those of Class II, but that are also capable of scaling and hence of progressively structuring the CA space. Class III CAs have proved to be good models of how the basic function of metabolism is carried out in similar ways in organisms of very different sizes (from oxen to squirrels). Finally Class IV systems are chaotic, that is unstable and random but with no predictable time limits (a Class IV CA, for example, is the weather where specific rules produce a high degree of randomness and unpredictability).

Artificial Life pioneer Chris Langton also attempted Wolfram's repeated runs of CA systems (this time running them thousands rather than hundreds of times). What he came up with was not only a different order of classification (I, II, IV and III), but also a key metric or lambda, which is correlated to the rate of information flow within a CA system. What lambda measures, that is, is the fluctuation of different CA systems with relation to their computational abilities. What Langton found was that this metric could vary between 0 (defining a state where a system is so random that it is incapable of computing) and 1 (defining a highly structured system that is not flexible enough to compute). A key finding was that the most interesting computational activity takes place at around the value of 0.5 – a value that within chaos theory is associated with phase transitions, that is with the points at which a system changes its state, such as for example when water starts to boil. Within CAs, then, the key area of computation is identified with a border zone fluctuating between highly ordered and highly random CAs. Within this phase, significantly, the behaviour of each node ceases to be strictly determined by its immediate neighbours and starts being affected by the overall fluctuation and propagation of information across the CA space. These fluid CAs have been shown to be capable of the most complex computation thus constituting a real alternative to Turing's universal machine, but one that does not respond to direct control.

SOCIAL EMERGENCE

The outcome of a CA run, then, cannot be predetermined or planned in its entirety (and as such, as Kevin Kelly put it, it is 'out of control'). Being out of control does not mean to be beyond control. The type of control that such fluid populations respond to, however, is quite different from the negative control of autopoietic living organisms that self-reproduce within closed boundaries. The fluidity of populations, their susceptibility to epidemics and contagion, is considered an asset: at a certain value or informational speed, the movement of cells turns liquid and it is this state that is identified as the most productive, engendering vortical structures that are both stable and propagating. It is these dynamic structures, as they are produced by the propagation of movement in a CA world, that are considered computationally interesting. This liquid behaviour is typically characterized by a swerve – that between the moment when the model is constructed, through a rule table and an initial configuration, and the moment of emergence of useful or pleasing forms. Ideally, CAs should always produce a level of surprise and unexpectedness for the human observer.

Getting CAs to compute, therefore, is no easy feat, for it requires a very careful fine tuning: the rules that define the transition functions between the different possible states of the cell must be determined with the utmost care. This fine tuning can only be carried out by successive runs until one is able to find the right computational level able to carry out a specific task. On the other hand, the fact that a CA system is in principle capable of carrying out a computation does not mean that it will actually do it spontaneously. This is why a new level of control is introduced – not just the fine tuning of initial conditions but also the modulation of the global aims and objects of the computation.

A common way in which such global modulation of aims is carried out in CA systems is through the 'genetic algorithm' model. Genetic algorithms are a special type of 'search algorithm', like the ones that run a popular search engines such as Google. Genetic algorithms work by searching the computational space and measuring the success rate of different CAs (defined by their genotypes or rule tables) on the basis of their phenotypes (that is the actual performance produced by the rules when starting from different configurations of the state of the nodes). What determines the outcome of the competition among CAs is a fitness function that defines the different scores attributed to different CAs. Inefficient CAs are screened out, while the most efficient systems are left to compete and even swap traits with each other. This model has proved to be highly effective in determining *optimal solutions* to specific problems, in as much as this CA race usually ends up by reaching an optimal zone where the task is computed efficiently and in a minimum amount of time. Successful genotypes, whose phenotypes have proved more successful than others, are thus selected for analysis or targeted use.

Genetic algorithms thus act as virtual sieves whose meshes can be adapted to the specific purposes of simulation. 'All that remains after this process is the cells that do not conform to the patterns and so form boundaries between the regions of cells that do.'[33] The behaviour of these active boundary particles is then analysed to see if it conforms to any kind of rule.

> If such a rule does exist (and can be found), then the CA has been explained ... If no such rule exists, then the process must be repeated, once again trying to extract patterns out of the mess of *particles* this time, yielding perhaps *meta-particles* and so on.[34]

The genetic algorithm approach to CAs has been criticized as being unable to produce *true emergence*, that is phenomena of self-organization and computation that are not explicitly programmed by a human agent. The genetic algorithm model of control is thus deemed insufficient by some ALife researchers in as much as it does not leave enough space to genuine emergence. If the fitness functions are too strict and too task-oriented, CAs can compute a task that has been given to them, but they cannot produce genuine novelty, that is events that are not prescribed by initial rules and conditions.[35] The genetic algorithm thus describes both a *mode of control and its limits* (those of 'true' emergence, that is of a potential for transformation that cannot be programmed or even aimed for).

The control of acentred multitudes thus involves different levels: the production of rule tables determining the local relations between neighbouring nodes; the selection of appropriate initial conditions; and the construction of aims and fitness functions that act like sieves within a liquid space, literally searching for the new and the useful. These sieves separate those configurations that seem to produce static outcomes from those dynamic particles that deviate the most from the structure. These dynamic particles do not obey laws of statistical regularity. Because they do not fall within the regular (or the ordinary) they can perform computations at the cutting edge. At the same time, these configurations cannot be allowed to pass all the way into randomness, where the turbulence is so strong that no real control can be exercised. The particles selected thus come to constitute a mobile and dynamic boundary zone or active limit capable of emergent computation. What the von Neumann machine reveals is a kind of content for a cybernetic machine of social control: not a fluctuating life threatened by entropic forces (as in the first cybernetic wave), but a level of indeterminate production entrusted to acentred multitudes that potentially never run out of energy. The content of such control is not a population understood as a mass that must be kept from undergoing dangerous swerves, but a multiplicity of computational milieus spread over a fluid and dynamical space.

HACKING THE MULTITUDE

In the late 1990s, the 'out of control' techniques of biological computations found particular favour with capitalist corporations, which have been important sponsors, for example, of the Artificial Life Center at the Santa Fe Institute. Cellular automata, in fact, model with a much greater degree of accuracy the chaotic fringes of the socius – zones of utmost mobility, such as fashions, trends, stock markets, and all distributed and acentred informational milieus. Biological computation parallels the emergence of a larger set of social techniques that are concerned with inducing and controlling the formation of bottom-up milieus of self-organization. Outside the computer medium, that is, biological computation expresses a socio-technical diagram of control that is concerned with producing effects of emergence by a manipulation of the rules and configurations within a given milieu.

If we were to look for human CA experiments, for example, we would find them in the organizational models of the New Economy, such as those documented by Andrew Ross's ethnography of New York's 'Silicon Alley' company Razorfish. For Ross, Razorfish, with its open-plan offices and its enthusiastic labour force who did not consider work as 'labour', constituted an important moment of experimentation with alternative modes of organization able to capitalize on the productive capacities of an educated and alienated GenX milieu. A dynamic and turbulent company that enjoyed an exponential expansion in the late 1990s, Razorfish was proud of its stimulating working environments that guaranteed a high level of innovation and professionalism in digital design. Razorfish's working environment, in its turn, expressed an encounter between the American East Coast bohemian profile and the Silicon Valley start-ups ecology – a highly successful model of a decentralized hotbed of technological innovations. In this sense, the social experiment of the New Economy, like biological computation itself, expressed an encounter between the innovative edges of the capitalist economy and the reflux of a 1960s counterculture and its rejection of dull and repetitive forms of labour.

Another description of the Razorfish offices by Lev Manovitch can further illustrate the point:

> The large, open space houses loosely positioned workspaces occupied mostly by twenty-something employees ... He [the manager] proudly points out that the workers are scattered around the open space regardless of their job titles – a programmer next to an interface designer next to a Web designer.[36]

Manovitch describes the space design as defined by computer culture's key themes 'interactivity, lack of hierarchy, modularity'. But these features are also those of the CA machines: a world without qualities, where all elements of a population are conceived exclusively from the point of view of local interactions with a view to the modulation of global aims and goals (such as staying on top of the digital design game). The work culture of the New Economy was informed by a movement of reform in management theory, which emphasized the value of letting teams of workers control the production process by introducing a new set of management rules (decentralization, delegation, deadline, etc.) The New Economy CA proved itself a highly turbulent and productive one, but was ultimately selected out of existence by the algorithms of a capitalism undergoing another of its energy crises. Whatever the fate of singular social CAs, biological computation is indicative of a mode in which the productivity of the milieu, as opposed to the territory, is highlighted: not a closed system (a people; a group; a class), but an open milieu (a dynamic multitude spreading across a smooth space).

Biological computing offers us an insight into a wider mode of soft control that takes as its focus the space–time of the swerve – that between the moment when the model is constructed, through the positioning of constraints and a local determination of behaviour, and the moment of emergence of useful or pleasing forms that are selected by exercising pressure or looked for through the elaboration of searching devices. Control is located at the two ends of the process: at the beginning, when a set of local rules is carefully put together and fine tuned; and at the end, when a searching device or a set of aims and objectives aim at ensuring the survival of the most useful or pleasing variations.

It is in this larger framework that we should understand the definition of a network offered by Kevin Kelly as 'the least structured organization that can be said to have any structure at all' but also 'one of the few structures that incorporates the dimension of time. It honors internal change. We should expect to see networks wherever we see constant irregular change, and we do.'[37] It is not just any network that will do to support the interaction of such large numbers, of this multitude in continuous variation. It is the network as a 'grand mesh', a form able to accommodate all variation and its mutations – an abstract machine that goes beyond the model to become the actual terrain for the study and engineering of complex and innovative behaviours. The open network is a global and large realization of the liquid state that pushes to the limits the capacity of control mechanisms effectively to mould the rules and select the aims: 'Running genetic mechanisms online puts heavy constraints on the selectionist mechanisms that can be used but it brings the experimental conditions closer to real autonomous robotic agents.'[38]

The great discovery of the biological turn is not only that there exists an abstract machine that can facilitate, contain and exploit the creative powers of a multitude (human and inhuman). It is also about the discovery of the immense *productivity* of a multitude, its absolute capacity to deterritorialize itself and mutate. What gives the biological turn its mystical tone, is the discovery of this productive line of flight, associated with the unpredictability of this middle zone, a relative autonomy and creativity, that is decoded, freed up from the constraints of sequential programming, almost at the same time as it is recoded, brought back into the fold by selection in the form of fitness functions. None of these considerations however takes away from the fact that a new content has entered the control of production: not simply a vague assemblage of information flows and feedback loops, but a spontaneously productive and autonomous force, endowed with its own specific activity that can be modelled and determined only at certain points, by exercising pressure selectively and moderately. Between local microdeterminism and the transcendental fitness functions, we find that the power of the middle zone can only be partially controlled. It is this middle, autonomous and productive zone, in between local determination and global selection, that the term 'emergence' partially captures.

One of the reasons why modelling emergence seems to be important is because it offers the key to a mode of control that does not require an absolute and total knowledge of all the states of each single component of the system or a rigid specification that rules behaviour exactly and sequentially. This new mode of control is 'soft', it applies a minimum amount of force, and modulates 'specification vs. creativity, closure and replicability vs. open-endedness and surprise'.[39] The abstract machine of soft control is thus concerned with fine tuning the local conditions that allow machines to outperform the designers' specifications, that surprise the designers but spontaneously improve on them, while also containing their possible space of mutation.

Thus, the founder of the Institute for Bionomics, for example, confidently argues for the necessity of abandoning the dependence of economic science on Newtonian physics.

> Where mainstream economics is based on concepts borrowed from classical Newtonian physics, bionomics is derived from the teachings of modern evolutionary biology. Where orthodox thinking describes the economy as a static, predictable engine, bionomics sees the economy as a self-organizing, 'chaotic' information ecosystem. Where the traditional view sees organizations as production machines, bionomics sees organizations as intelligent social organisms. Where conventional business strategy focuses on physical capital, bionomics holds that organizational learning is the ultimate source of all profit and growth.[40]

We have come to associate such statements with a short-lived phase of capitalist euphoria, but notions of bottom-up organization of large numbers within fluid spaces are still central categories in our apprehension of a medium such as the Internet. To many, in fact, the strange behaviour of the Internet, especially its capacity to expand and mutate with no plan and no central controller in charge, has appeared uncannily lifelike. The Internet as a medium and a culture appears to many as a macroscopic demonstration of the existence and feasibility of acentred and leaderless forms of organization that mirror some of those that we are familiar with in the natural world. After all, the Internet mainly developed as a parallel, piecemeal, localized activity, so that it can be classified, according to Sadie Plant for example, as 'bottom-up'.[41] Electronic Frontier Foundation pioneer Jon Gilmore's claim to immortality is probably to have coined the sentence: 'The Net interprets censorship as damage and routes around it.'[42]

This catchy statement, a refrain of network culture, is grounded in important technical features of the Internet and guaranteed by a socio-technical culture that similarly emphasizes autonomous and distributed forms of organization of labour. The popularity of peer-to-peer networks, open-source software or recent phenomena such as web logs is only the most recent example of what seems to many an intrinsic vitality of a bottom-up, piecemeal, parallel approach to organization and the culture that it supports. This spontaneous productivity is said to be intrinsically related to the distributed and decentralized organization of large numbers of interacting peers and to be a feature of social, technical and natural systems. It is an *excessive* production of cooperation and interaction that has brought forth the development of new techniques of control.

Does this imply, then, that the Internet as a medium and as a cultural multiplicity by virtue of its loose, bottom-up technical structure, has managed to replicate some of the features of the natural world? The description of the Internet as an ecosystem, inhabited by knowledge, and substantially self-organizing was common in the mid 1990s, when neoliberal and conservative writers such as Alvin Toffler, George Gilder, Esther Dyson and Newt Gingrich used it to forcefully reject the Clinton administration's description of cyberspace as an 'information superhighway'.[43] In *Being Digital*, Nicholas Negroponte, popular columnist on *Wired* and director of the Media Lab at MIT, similarly considered the Internet to be a remarkable 'example of something that has evolved with no apparent designer in charge, keeping its shape very much like the formation of a flock of ducks.'[44]

Controversy around such statements marked the 'California ideology' wars of the early 1990s, controversies that pitted the techno-utopianism of Californian hippy entrepreneurs against the critical objections of sociologists and cultural activists. The controversy around the self-organising and lifelike nature of the Internet split the 1990s cybercultures along neat ideological lines. Such an opposition could be possible in an atmosphere where social scientists and humanities scholars had mostly aligned themselves with a radical social constructionism, according to which nothing social can also be natural. Starting from the notion that everything that is natural is fixed and predetermined, many writers rejected the analogy between the Internet and natural systems on the basis of the idea (often justified) that such statements implied a kind of neo-social Darwinism. To say that the Internet might be lifelike was the equivalent of sanctioning the ravages brought by rampant free-market capitalism on the 'excluded' masses.

But wasn't somehow such an exclusive and often vehement rejection of 'natural metaphors' and 'analogies' as they were called missing something as well? The notion that the Internet presented features and behaviours that could also be observed amongst natural phenomena was not simply a set of statements meant to organize the perception that gave social form to a new medium. The study of lifelike behaviour, in fact, is not simply a rhetorical exercise but has been accompanied by a larger move that connects social to natural and technical components. The biological turn is, as we have seen, not simply a new approach to computation, but it also aspires to offer a social technology of control able to explain and replicate not only the collective behaviour of a distributed network such as the Internet, but also the complex and unpredictable patterns of contemporary informational capitalism. Thus, the simulation of the behaviour of 'a multitude of simultaneous actions' is also seen as the key to understanding not only the behaviour of stock markets, but also that of 'fashion and fads'.[45]

The biological turn thus seems to extend from computing itself towards a more general conceptual approach to understanding the dynamic behaviour of the Internet, network culture, milieus of innovation and contemporary 'deregulated' markets – that is of all social, technical and economic structures that are characterized by a distributed and dynamic interaction of large numbers of entities with no central controller in charge. These systems are not unstructured or formless, but they are *minimally structured* or *semi-ordered.* Since the turbulent flow of information ensuing from a 'multitude of nonlinear simultaneous actions' is not exclusive to the Internet and market economies, but can also be observed in a variety of natural phenomena, then it is quite appropriate that this specific potential of the natural world should become the object of intense technical, cultural and economic interest. The 'business network' of the Institute for Complexity in Santa Fe, for example, includes Citibank/Citicorp, Coca-Cola, Hewlett-Packard, Intel, Interval, John

Deere, Shell International B.V., Xerox and a variety of financial advising companies. 'Early on, the CEO of Citibank/Citicorp became interested in SFI and helped begin SFI's program in understanding the world economy as a complex evolving system.'[46]

Any discussion of the Internet as a lifelike phenomenon seems thus to be entangled with the reformulation of the problem of *control,* in terms which are more appropriate to the behaviour of the new entities that contemporary scientific and technological research are literally discovering, as Ilya Prigogine put it, after years of neglect: open systems subject to a large variety of semi-autonomous variables. Control here is cybernetically defined in two ways: as the opposite of mechanical rationality (step-by-step programming), because the latter is too rigid and ultimately too brittle to operate on such terrain; and also as the antithesis of centralized government, because the latter presupposes a complete knowledge of each individual component of the overall system, which is impossible to achieve in these types of structure.

Taylorism and governmentality are thus both rejected as unsuited to this new turbulent, but also hugely productive terrain. At the same time, however, cybernetic control as defined by the first wave of cybernetics, that associated with the work of Norbert Wiener, is also rejected. It no longer sufficient to neutralize all positive feedback, that is all new variations and mutations, by bringing the system back to a state of equilibrium (negative control is acknowledged as ultimately ineffective in staving off the forces of chaos). The open and productive systems studied by the biological turn are, by definition, always operating in far-from-equilibrium conditions, dynamically perched between two layers and conditions: one rigid, unmovable and ultimately sterile, associated with permanence and stasis; and another chaotic and turbulent, opening up onto unexpected and potentially catastrophic transformations. The problem of contemporary modes of control is to steer the spontaneous activities of such systems to plateaus that are desirable and preferable. What we seem to have then is the definition of a new biopolitical plane that can be organized through the deployment of an *immanent control,* which operates directly within the productive power of the multitude and the clinamen.

THE UNHAPPY GENE

It seems then, as if the science of multitudes has definitely given up on the individual, which it dismisses as an epiphenomenon that is simply too coarse and rigid to be more than a by-product of emergence. If there is an abstract social machine of soft control, it takes as its starting point the productivity of an acentred and leaderless multitude. However, we might also say of the individual what Michel Foucault said of the family in his analysis of the rise of governmentality in the modern state. Talking about the new place of the family in the mode of governmentality, Foucault comments that the family disappears as a model but is kept as a tool of government. We could say a similar thing for the development of soft control. The new place of the individual in the mode of immanent control is not as a *model* for the organization of a multitude, but as a *tool* that allows the overcoding and the ultimate containment of the productive power of flows. To the decoding of the mass into a network culture, to the dissolution of the individual into the productive powers of a multitude, corresponds an over-coding of the multitude onto the individual element understood as a unit of code modelled on the biological notion of the gene.

Among the mixture of disciplinary insights drawn upon by biological computing, in fact, we find the controversial thesis of sociobiological thinkers such as Richard Dawkins, author of pop science bestsellers such as *The Selfish Gene*, *The Blind Watchmaker*, and *River Out of Eden*. To simplify Dawkins' work somewhat, we might say that he understands the variations of populations as ultimately determined by the 'selfish' drive of individual genes. This selfish drive compels them to replicate themselves at the expense of other competing genes. The human body, or for that matter the whole of the world of organic and inorganic life, is simply about the set of devices through which selfish genes manage to replicate and protect themselves by competing with other genes in an environment characterized by scarce resources. Dawkins himself experimented with biological computation (and he wrote about it in *The Blind Watchmaker*).

The concept of the selfish gene is crucial to biological computing, and therefore relevant to our understanding of soft control. It is here not simply a matter of ideological affinity between the white male milieu of Alife researchers (as described by Stephen Helmreich) and the sociobiological perspective. It is not so much, in fact, that biological computing is influenced by sociobiology, as that they both share a keen understanding of the necessity of introducing some kind of 'cut' in the fluid fabric of a population for the purposes of artificial synthesis of the computational capacities of natural life. In this sense, sociobiological work such as Dawkins' does not so much inform as clarify the modalities according to which the individual is given a new role to play within the open plane of emergence.

Dawkins defines a gene in computational terms as 'a sequence of nucleotide letters lying between a START and an END symbol and coding for one protein chain'.[47] What characterizes this unit is its capacity to replicate itself and to survive through a large number of successive individual copies.[48] There is no fixed measure for such units:

> I am using the word gene to mean a genetic unit that is small enough to last for a large number of generations and to be distributed around in the form of many copies. This is not a rigid all-or-nothing definition, but a kind of fading-out definition, like the definition of 'big' or 'old'. The more likely a length of chromosome is to be split by crossing-over, or altered by mutations of various kinds, the less it qualifies to be called a gene in the sense in which I am using this term.[49]

This unit is endowed with a minimum set of capacities: the capacity to replicate itself, where replication is a kind of *dynamic mobility*, because by replicating, genes also tend to mutate; the capacity to compete for scarce resources; and the capacity to collaborate, but only if collaboration suits the selfish aims of the gene, that is its freedom of replication.

> What I have done is to define a gene as a unit which, to a high degree, *approaches* the ideal of indivisible particulateness. A gene is not indivisible, but it is seldom divided. It is either definitely present or definitely absent in the body of any given individual.[50]

What Dawkins' theory allows is the replacement of the individual by the unit or, as Deleuze named it, a 'dividual' resulting from a 'cut' within the polymorphous and yet nondeterministic mutations of a multitude.[51] Dawkins is very explicit in defining the individual as an unsuitable basic unity for the kind of giant computational capabilities that underlie the evolutionary process. It is not a matter of immortality, because individual genes or units of code are not immortal. They have emerged at some times out of the chemical interactions of a turbulent matter–energy continuum and will die eventually, even if their lifespan can be measured in thousands or even millions of years. Genes, however, are not individuals but units in the sense that they do not grow senile, they are never young or old, that is they are not subjected to the second law of thermodynamics that decrees that the individual organism is bound to die and decay. As informational units, all that matters is their capacity to replicate themselves and survive in their many copies – or fail in replicating successfully and hence disappear. In this sense, the life of a unit is binary: it is either there or not there; it does not grow any older or younger with time; it is a cut in the body of the multitude that makes it more manageable from the point of view of the replicability and synthesis of a specific type of control diagram.

Dawkins' formulation of the gene is thus perfectly suitable to find its application in the biological turn, because it defines genes by means of the cut that gives a program a functional beginning and an end. The computational abilities of the gene unit are not constructed or attributed by Dawkins to the gene, but, on the basis of contemporary scientific knowledge and research, they have been shown to correspond to some of the capacities of genetic molecules. They have also provided the basic concept through which the biological turn has managed to translate these ideas into actual working pieces of software, that are capable of producing their own emergent phenomena. In this sense and at its most basic level, Dawkins' understanding of the gene is of genuine relevance to any attempt at modelling natural laws in a technical machine. If a gene is a unit of code, that is identifiable as lying between two symbols, one designating Start and the other End, then it can be easily coded by a computer. If one writes several units of codes and lets them be free to pursue their survival by replication, they will at some point manifest different degrees of emergent behaviour. At the level of simulation, identifying a unit of code as an individual allows better manipulation, and greatly enhances the possibility of determining and applying local rules of behaviour. It also allows the identification of units that can be rewarded and/or punished, selected and/or rejected.

Biological computing suggests that the bounded organism contains both the pre-individual and the collective – two levels of being that are infinitely more productive than the individual as such. They are more productive because they do not produce *thermodynamically*, like the organism, for example, that burns heat and progressively drives itself to a slow decay and finally death. As we have seen, units of code are mortal, but they do not grow old. They are either there or

not there and when they are there they are always productive, always
doing something.

The most common critique to Dawkins' theory from sociologists
and cultural theorists is that this little unit of code is classified as
'selfish', that is juxtaposed with a category that belongs to very
different planes of organization – those of a Protestan–capitalist
apparatus of subjectification.[52] Why should a unit of code be subjected
to the moral universe of good and evil, which is where 'selfishness'
and 'altruism' are located? In the passage from the description of the
gene as a unit of code and the unconvincing description of the gene
as 'selfish' like a 'trade unionist', or a 'Chicago Gangster', something
else happens. The unit of code that we know as the gene has been
returned to individuality so that it might assume the attributes of
selfishness and altruism, competition and collaboration. The mode
of existence of the selfish gene (the individual) as opposed to the
'gene' (unit of code; genetic algorithm) is the distance that separates
the simulation of molecular life and the capture of the powers of a
multitude in a network culture. If the gene is a unit of code that
makes evolution a computing machine, the selfish gene is the
subjectifying function that turns a multitude into an assemblage of
isolated individuals.

The selfishness of the subject of informational capitalism which
is the underlying metaphor here has little to do with actual genes.
As Dawkins himself admits, genes have no 'purposes', they obey
obscure impulses dictated by complex chemical laws. With no sense
of purpose, arguably, there is no self and hence no selfishness. What
the term 'selfishness' does, however, is to betray some of the ways
in which the social powers of the multitude are captured. Selfishness
is defined by Dawkins as a sociobiological tension between competition
and collaboration – where the gene is like a calculating machine
always weighing the advantages of collaborating or competing in
order to gain an advantage of survival. If the selfish gene is a subject,
it is because it thinks, and it can think only two thoughts: in a
particular situation, do I increase my chances of survival by
collaborating with other units? Or am I better off looking after
number one to the exclusion of and in competition with others?
Selfishness closes the open space of a multitude down to a hole of
subjectification.

The selfish gene is a simple diagram of the apparatuses of
subjectification that the abstract machine of soft control distributes
and perpetuates not so much among molecules as among collectivities.

Television, as the culturally sensitive medium that it is, has been quick to pick up and amplify these mechanisms in ways which complement our analysis of soft control in the biological turn. Reality TV games such as *Big Brother*, *Survivor*, *Desert Island*, and *Pop Idol* dramatize the schizoid tensions that emerge when the subject is placed within an abstract machine that requires the coexistence of competition and collaboration under the aegis of selfishness. There has been much talk about how the New Economy turned around the classic Malthusian emphasis on scarcity in order to promote the unlimited promise of abundance of the digital domain. Within reality TV games, we find some of the outlines of the peculiar forms of post-scarcity competition, and their psychic drives, that are widespread in informational capitalist cultures.

Reality games can be seen as cellular automata that operate by capturing a segment of the audience within a space that is both closed (a house, a competition) and open (subjected to the whims of ratings and popular votes). As such they demand the impossible from their willing participants: that they relinquish their individuality by being forced to interact continuously with a group which will decide their fate (hence they must become a unit ready for selection); that they relinquish their privacy by being continuously placed under the surveillance gaze of a camera; and, at the same time, that they hold onto and reinforce such individuality as part of the competitive structure of punishments and rewards of the game. They demand then a self that is stripped down to the capacity to collaborate and compete by a strict set of rules operating within an economy of punishments and rewards, which determine the persistence or disappearance of the self as such. The group dynamics that are engendered by the distribution of the space, the set of initial conditions, the state of the cells within the system (the contestants), and the rules applied by a transcendent entity (Big Brother's voice ...) produce a kind of 'emergent entertainment'. In reality game shows, the competition is, at an immediate level, for the prize that only one of the contenders will be able to gain. More fundamentally, however, the competition is for the fleeting, rather than scarce, flow of the audience's attention and sympathy that from the outside keep impinging on the game and repeatedly push it towards a claustrophobic instability. Franco Berardi has accurately described some of the effects of these contradictory pressures on the informational subjectivities as the 'unhappiness factory'.[53]

It is understandable, then, that rebellion to the claustrophobic selfishness structure (with its two poles of competition and collaboration) should be explicitly marked by the *rejection* of being subjectified as selfish genes striving for survival at the expense of others. The most challenging areas of network culture in terms of control are those that emerge out of a choice for the chemical interaction of relationships of affinity and/or war within a space that is radically open over that of selfishness/cooperation within a close subjectivity structure. Not altruism against selfishness, but relationships of affinity and war (a wholly different economy of relations) that cut through the space of the individual without reducing it to a unit – but freeing up a potential for transformation and even catastrophe. From the point of view of the abstract machine of soft control, there is no ontological difference between the threat of a global network of terrorists able to carry out devastating attacks on the heart of empire and the threat of a global network of anticapitalist activists (hence the recurrent and contested claims, after 11 September, that the movement for global justice was potentially terrorist), or the behaviour of connected peers exchanging copyrighted files without payment on peer-to-peer networks. I am not implying that they are all the same, of course, or that the punishments can be compared. The potentials for destruction and creation are also very differently weighted. But from the perspective of this mode of cybernetic control they do express different sides of the same rebellion: the rejection of the existential condition of living as a stripped down selfish gene, endowed with the intoxicating capacity to form a multitude, but recoded within the claustrophobic black hole of the selfishness structure (cooperation/ competition). The threat of these swerves, from the perspective of the engineers of control, is that by rejecting the system's most basic sets of constraints, by rejecting the micromoulding of dividualism, they might push it out of control, towards a new plateau, whose outcome not only cannot be predetermined but might also veer the system violently towards catastrophic transformations.

There is a big gap, of course, between the small pieces of code that we know as genetic algorithms and cellular automata, and the dynamics of political resistance in network societies – a gap that actualizes itself in divergence and turbulence. The selfish gene, however, is not just a metaphor, or a moralization of natural life or an ideological justification of cut-throat competition in the 'free' market economy, but *more insidiously* a technique. It is a mode of capture of value produced by an increasingly interconnected and interdependent culture in as much as the latter is also an industry – and hence a mode of labour. This excessive value that can never be really reabsorbed in a logic of exchange and equivalence is frequently referred to in autonomist Marxist writings as a kind of biopower of labour – that is a power of making and remaking the world through the reinvention of life. That nothing could be further away and yet so close to the models of biological computation says something about the political stakes involved in the emergence (and control) of network societies.

CODA ON SOFT CONTROL

If we open up a path for critical inquiry and conceptual engagement with biological computation beyond the deconstructive critique, are we necessarily playing the game of power, that is accepting the naturalization of social relations? In a way, we are, in the sense that we accept that the game of power is the only game in town in as much as it identifies and enacts an *indetermination* of the social and the natural across a microphysical continuum that denies the human the ontological status of an exception. On the other hand, beyond the easy rhetoric of popular accounts of self-organization, the natural that emerges out of biological computing is as artificial as the social – indeed it is the artificiality of the natural that the social takes over and reinvents.

In this sense, biological computing opens up two interesting questions for a cultural politics of network culture. On the one hand, it challenges us to think about how a certain mode of distributed organization can become also the milieu for the development of new modes of control. Thus it takes the notion of self-regulation and organization in large numbers outside any mythological landscape of a utopia to be realized and places it firmly within the horizon of emerging modes of power. Self-organization, in other words, is not incompatible with transcendent control or with the 'unhappiness factory' assembled by informational capitalism.

On the other hand, and more intriguingly, an engagement with biological computation and the sciences of emergence offers us a way to engage with the political concept of the 'multitude' beyond the temptation of reconstituting a new, indefinite subject of history. As defined by Hardt and Negri in *Empire*, and as adopted within the activist milieus of network culture, a multitude defines a political mode of engagement that is located outside the majoritarian and representative model of modern democracies in their relation with the recomposition of class experience. Unlike class, however, a multitude is not rooted in a solid class formation or a subjectifying function (although it is also a matter of class composition). It is too indefinite a concept to carry such power. For Franco Berardi, '[t]he notion of the multitude describes a tendency to dissolution, the entropy that is diffused in every social system and which renders impossible ('asintotico,' infinite, interminable) the labour of power but also the labour of political organisation'.[54] Like the smooth milieus of biological computation, the multitude too is a necessarily vague term that is defined mainly by a fluidity of movement and by the formations that such fluidity leaves behind as a kind of after-effect. As such, it does not deny the existence of the stratifications of identity and class, but it opens up another dimension where such positions are caught in terms of other types of capacity. If this is the case, then biogical computation (in its widest possible sense) is an attempt to 'hack the multitude' – to hack the social at its most fluid and least stratified, wherever it escapes the constrictions of rigid forms of organization but also of identity and class. As such and beyond some of its most simplistic applications, the CA model has much to offer to any attempt to think about processes of bottom-up organization and emergence in network culture, their relationship to the reorganization of capitalist modes of production and the political potentials that such reorganization opens up. Hacking the multitude is still an open game.

5
Communication Biopower

In his bestselling critical account of his time as the chief economist and senior vice-president of the World Bank, Joseph Stiglitz repeatedly suggests that one of the problems with international institutions is their lack of transparency and hence accountability. The systematic manner in which the International Monetary Fund managed effectively to undermine growth in developing countries and enrich foreign investors was for him a result of a culture of secrecy in which the actions of the Fund were not subject to a sustained public scrutiny (whilst also being skewed in favour of US lobbies' economic interests).

> Secrecy also undermines democracy. There can be democratic accountability only if those to whom these public institutions are supposed to be accountable are well informed about what they are doing – including what choices they confronted and how those decisions were made.[1]

Thus for Stiglitz, freedom of information is paramount and 'sunshine is the best antiseptic', that is exposure of such dealings to the light of public opinion is conducive to healing the malaise of international governance. Or, as it has also been put, within a one-world power system, 'public opinion is the new superpower'.

In asking for more transparency and better accountability, Stiglitz is echoing one of the most fundamental assumptions of modern political thought, in which the relationship between transparency of communication and democracy is foundational.[2] From Diderot and Voltaire to Thomas Payne, modern conceptions of democracy start from the demands of bourgeois revolutionaries for free speech and political representation. A democracy does not just guarantee but *is guaranteed by* the rights of its citizens to representation in the spheres of both politics and communication. These rights include that of accessing information concerning the exercise of public authority (as expressed for example in the US Freedom of Information Act (1966)) and that to have one's position represented in the spectrum of positions. Freedom of information and communication sustains freedom of speech and freedom of speech supports democracy. Without access to a public space of information and communication, citizens would not be able to learn how the *res publica* is run, to develop informed opinions, and to express them and exercise pressures on governments. Without a public space in which to express and communicate ideas and form a shared opinion, there is no democracy.[3]

In *The Structural Transformation of the Public Sphere*, Jürgen Habermas outlined the original model for such a conception of the relationship between communication and the political – the bourgeois public sphere emerging in Western Europe in the late eighteenth century. Habermas defines the bourgeois public sphere as a distinctive space where private individuals assemble to form a public body. 'They then behave neither like business or professional people transacting private affairs, nor like members of a constitutional order subject to the legal constraints of a state bureaucracy.'[4] As constituted within a public space of communication (such as the press, clubs and societies of eighteenth-century Europe), the public mediates between constituted power, that is the state and its institutions, and the private autonomous interests of free economic agents. A political public sphere is based on freedoms of assembly and association, including the freedom to express and make public one's opinions.

For Habermas, in its early manifestations when it coincided with the emergence of the bourgeoisie as an ascending class, the public sphere allowed an independent space from where to 'rationalize' the public exercise of authority. Thus the public 'transforms political into rational authority within the medium of the public sphere'. Public opinion accepts that the power of government must be delegated, but it reserves the right to check and monitor the actions of politicians. 'In a large public body, this kind of communication requires specific means for transmitting information and influencing those who receive it.'[5] At the same time, the overwhelming power of the media in the political life of social democracies has led some to argue that the media have now become the 'new public sphere'. This mediation of politics by the media in mass democracies has been a constant motif of crisis for the liberal axis linking communication to reason and progress.[6] It is as if communication had been returned to a pre-Enlightenment mode – that of the spectacle, gossip and manipulation which are seen as *undermining* reason, rather than being a medium for its expression.

The relationship between communication and democracy has never actually been the exclusive domain of a 'public sphere' in which citizens can monitor the action of elected and accountable governments. Communication has never only been about the sunshine of reason illuminating the dark secrets of governance, but it has always cast its own shadows – those of a manipulation that takes as its object the blind passions of the masses. At least since the totalitarian regimes of the mid twentieth century proved the power of mass communication, the relationship between communication and the political has been a murky affair that cannot but puzzle enlightened reason. It has become impossible to ignore the way in which much communication is not simply about access to information and public debate, but is also about manipulation by way of positive (spin, propaganda, hegemony) and negative tactics (censorship, exclusion, distortion, etc.). The impossible task of the public sphere thus becomes that of returning communication to an older, purer function by combating the corrupting influence of manipulation, censorship, propaganda and spin. However, this activity would be pointless if this public sphere did not aim to represent and address an inherently interested and enlightened public to whose opinion governments are bound. If such reasonable public opinion was shown not to exist or to be ineffectual in influencing the actions of politicians, then the organs of public opinion would lose much of their power.

The problem is that this entity, this public which is deemed to exist somewhere at the end of the communication process, those citizens/audiences/readers, often do not seem to embody the qualities of the 'enlightened citizen' at all. Media power, specifically the power of the mass media, appears as partially incompatible with the eighteenth century's model of political communication. How else to explain the fact that it is predominantly populist and/or authoritarian voices that seem to be almost natural masters of the mediascape? How does one explain right-wing talk-show hosts, Ronald Reagan, Margaret Thatcher, tele-evangelists and tele-marketeers, Silvio Berlusconi, George W. Bush, *Pop Idol*, Osama bin Laden and Tony Blair?

The most common way to explain all of the above (with all due respect to the differences), is to point out how material access and control of the media is restricted to those who can afford it. The centrality of communication to political life has made a massive investment into media culture by corporate actors and institutional parties both rational and inevitable. It is simply a matter of capital expenditure: it pays off to control the media, and after all, if you have money and power, access to the media almost comes automatically. Communication and media culture reproduce the opinions of their owners and it is no wonder that they should support conservative ideological formations. With control of the media firmly in the hands of the ruling classes, the masses can be seduced into a consensus. Whether it is about TV tycoons turned politicians or about direct political control of the media by corporate lobbies, communication is today deemed to be driven by private interests and thus on the whole to be unabashedly manipulative and openly populist. The domination of our mediasphere by gossip, celebrities, fashion, salesmen, propagandists and special effects is thus a signal of this 'perversion of communication'.

The manipulation of public opinion today is no amateur business but is a field of systematic research, corresponding to the development of specific techniques that make the formation of hegemonic consensus an affair for professionals.[7] Thus, the public sphere of the welfare state and mass democracy is described by Habermas in terms that are markedly different from those of the bourgeois public sphere. While the bourgeois public sphere comprises individuals engaged in public discussion, within mass democracy, the state and private interests are directly involved, as the pressure on journalists and the aggressively televisual nature of politics demonstrates. The current public sphere is not a sphere of mediation between state and civil society, but the site of a permanent conflict, informed by strategies of media warfare. Communication is not a space of reason that mediates between the state and society, but is now a site of direct struggle between the state and different organizations representing the private interests of organized groups of individuals. The corruption of communication that many see at the heart of the corruption of democratic life is thus blamed on the illegitimate interference of private interests in the public sphere. But if this is the case, and considering the entrenched interests that rule the media industry with ferocious determination and expansionist aims, and the passivity of the masses, can communication be saved at all? And if not, how do we switch it off?

THE MASSES' ENVELOPMENT

There is always another solution of course. If communication has been 'corrupted' by private interests, the argument goes, then the reconstitution of a free and open space of communication should be a key force in driving the return of a more authentic democratic life. If the worst danger to democratic life today is the political and oligopolistic control of the media system, then a new medium of communication that would be somehow free of this 'old media' baggage is extremely important. It is on these foundations that the hopes for 'new media' (and more specifically the Internet) were laid. As soon as the Internet started to materialize as a set of relays and links between different computer networks, it produced a widespread and hopeful expectation of a resurgence of the public sphere in a 'cyberdemocratic mode'. A networked multitude, possessing its own means of communication, freed from the tyranny of broadcasting, would rise to challenge the phony public sphere of television and the press. Since then, the Internet, as we shall see, has proved to be an effective political medium in terms of its power of mobilization and the openness of its information space. It has thus made visible the existence of a global networked mass with a stake in regional, national and global political processes. At the same time as such masses have appeared on the global mediasphere, however, the problem has become that of the *other mass,* the silent majority, the television public held hostage by the powerful media monopolies in a topsy-turvy world of propaganda and simulation.

It is not so much a question here of opposing a good, networked mass with a bad, couch-potato mass (there are plenty of couch potatoes on the Internet). It is rather about understanding what kind of relation might exist between these two formations as they are given to us within the sphere of communication. The political category of the mass, or even that of the silent majority, is not very popular within media and cultural studies – which, from Raymond Williams onwards, has tended to identify it with a kind of conservative modernity, apopulist and thus implicitly anti-working class. It was also one of Jean Baudrillard's most unsettling propositions (at least for his critics), that the masses do not need or want a 'political–intellectual class' (including activists and critics) to teach them how to avoid manipulation by the media or to coalesce behind another consensus. On the contrary, for Baudrillard, one should always keep in mind that the masses are a stronger medium than the media and that the masses have never been on the side of reason, to which they always preferred the seductive power of the spectacle – whether of gladiators' fights, public executions, sports, games, ceremonies, fireworks or special effects. For Baudrillard the media do not manipulate the masses, but it is the masses who 'envelop the media' because they are themselves already a medium.

Indeed it does seem at times as if the media manipulation by spin doctors, cultural populists and public relations officers were actually giving in to a disturbing request, coming from somewhere on the other side of the camera and the screen. The power that is formed by a mass or that gives rise to a mass is amorphous and demanding, always implicated in the rise of a desire that demands *distraction* – more and better images; better and bigger effects. For Baudrillard, the spectacularization of communication, and hence the spectacularization of politics, is thus not imposed on the masses, but demanded by the formation of a mass. The masses are not specific social classes, but more of a generalized dynamics that takes over when you take away all attributes, predicates, qualities or references from a large number of people. The mass, that is, is a lowest common denominator, not in the sense of a loss of quality but as a kind of pre-individual and collective potential to be affected. This is about the physical capacity of a large number of bodies to form a kind of passive mass – a receptacle for the affective power of images. No longer the mass congealed and energized by the containment strategies of the industrial revolution and its disciplinary enclosures, but a kind of terminal mass – atomized and dispersed at the end of communication receivers, deprived of its revolutionary power in a kind of entropic dispersion.

In Baudrillard's astute analysis of the mass, however, the latter retains throughout its history a kind of passive power – that of excess. Baudrillard's own example is that of medicine: the medicalization of life devised as a means of chemical control of the masses' bodies is pushed to the extreme by patients' demands for more and more drugs: 'an excessive, uncontrollable consumption of medicine, a panicked conformity to health injunctions'.[8] We might imagine Baudrillard's take on the recent vicissitudes of the stock market. Look at what happened when the masses entered the market, he might say. They demanded more stocks, larger and quicker profits, and they almost broke it! They inflated the market, causing it to crash. The hyperconformity of the masses did not spare anybody: CEOs and regular employees; small and large investors; investment firms and national governments; directors of national banks and private investors. As a result of the entry of the masses into the New Economy, the whole stock market went through an unsustainable acceleration until it crashed.[9] If one really thought it through, a public sphere, understood as the space of free formation of public opinion, would be incompatible with mass democracy. Wherever there is a mass, there is the preponderance of an economy of spectacles, hyperconformity and excess.

It would be easy to 'correct' Baudrillard's provocations by pointing out that there is a good deal of speculation going on, both in the pharmaceutical and in the financial industry; and that in the end, it was the small investors who paid dearly for some cynical operations performed by large investment banks. Or we might object that such an understanding of the masses is aristocratic in nature and does not do justice to the active relationship between individuals and media power. On the other hand, such arguments would miss the point of Baudrillard's challenge. What his understanding of the masses or the silent majority explains is a certain quality of communication that is usually perceived as a problem of media societies, at least from the perspective of a modern conception of politics based on the exercise of reason within a transparent public sphere. Baudrillard's argument could be reinterpreted to indicate that the powerful presence of the masses, or of silent majorities, in mainstream media or in mass democracies poses a repeated problem for postmodern political thinking. This problem is that of imaging a 'political without the social' – if we understand the masses as a nonsociological category, a category that does not possess any social qualifications such as class or gender or ethnicity or even a geographical place. Understood in this sense, as a political entity with no social foundations (either in the relations of production or in the economy of gender or ethnicity or race), the mass appears as an inertial force and a zone of implosion of social energies. (As the a.f.r.i.k.a group put it in a posting to the mailing list *nettime*, 'Everybody knows that the Ozone belt is fading away. Everybody knows that the rich are getting richer and the poor are getting poorer ...'.)[10]

At the same time, however, this asocial quality of the masses is what makes it a crucial entry point into another relation between communication and the political – beyond and beneath the play of reason. Baudrillard calls the moment when the masses take over the zero degree of the political, the moment where the spectacle meets 'the grey eminence of politics'. The paradox is that such zero degree of the political is defined as the moment when society has reached a stage of maximum socialization – where everything has become social, that is mediated, signified and subjectified. For social and cultural theory, in fact, in order to become a subject, in order to be able to act, we must first be 'socialized' – that is our raw subjective experience must be made social. We are socialized when we learn who we are and where we belong by acknowledging and internalizing our place in the great differential grid of society. We are socialized when we learn about the difference between self and other, subject and object, between the way 'we' are (women, white, children, workers, managers, abuse survivors, single mothers, single men, etc.) and the way 'they' are (men, black, adults, capitalists, workers, abusers, husbands, single women, etc). Socialization implies the intervention of mediations and signifying chains in the formation of subjectivity. We become what we are by assuming a role that is defined for us by another subject – that is somebody who re-presents and makes that role meaningful to us. However, for theorists of late modernity from Fredric Jameson to Anthony Giddens, these images, beckoning to us, asking us to identify with them, have simply become too many (the mirror of the social has multiplied in a fun-house effect). From every side, the social demands our attention.

Socialization thus implies an overproduction of meaning, a state of always being told and asked too much. It is a matter of having been told too many truths and too many opinions and perspectives so that communication ceases to be representational and becomes tactical and strategic. It does not simply represent and make meaningful, but it shifts, it touches and it commands. This situation has not just produced a state of 'reflexivity', where we continually police ourselves trying to produce the right identity, but also a state of being a mass, the relief of being in a mass. Masses ('you, me and everybody else') are thus not definite sociological categories like classes. The masses are everywhere and in everybody in as much as they lie at the points where all mediations have collapsed and meaning no longer takes hold. The masses are the place where meanings and ideas lose their power of penetration, the place of fascination and dismediation where all statements, opinions and ideas flow through without leaving a mark. The masses 'disperse' and 'diffuse' meaning, and this is their political power.

Baudrillard is not really implying here that people do not understand media messages or that they do not make meanings with them. He acknowledges that from the point of view of individuals and groups, we still have resistant readings of media messages, such as, for example, when a group decodes a message by translating it into its own code in acts of frontal resistance (trade unionists listening to the official news of a strike; ethnic minorities listening to mainstream media coverage, etc.) What appears more relevant, however, is that the overall effects of all these little acts often end up being dispersed in the mass domain. When seen from the perspective of government, that is of the macropolitical control of majorities, the masses are always constituted as silent. If they communicate at all, it is by way of focus groups and opinion polls in a language of forever fluctuating and often contradictory percentages. In this emergence of the masses as a statistical source, Baudrillard would argue, there is not just the mass's manipulation, but also its complicity. Hence his uncomfortable hypothesis that the centrality of meaning formation and the exchange of ideas to political life are mainly the sites of investment by a 'political class' (including critical intellectuals) who needs them to justify their existence.

> The political sphere also only survives by a credibility hypothesis, namely that the masses are permeable to action and discourse, that they hold an opinion, that they are present behind the surveys and statistics. It is at this price alone that the political class can still believe that it speaks and that it is politically heard.[11]

The question, then, is not that the public sphere has been corrupted by private interests or even by the contamination of images. There is no inherent condemnation of the visual in favour of speech and writing; on the contrary. Images are always predominant in the formation and emergence of a mass and the mass is not only survey material, but also a kind of 'zero degree of the political', that is the moment where the political starts again, as from a zero degree or a state of fullness and potential. For Baudrillard, the degree zero of the political is the moment of maximum depoliticization, the moment when the social and its mediation appear to have exhausted the play of social forces, when everything appears as a representation and representation becomes a hyperreality. At the same time, however, such a point of absolute socialization is also seen as a turning point, the moment when the political makes its comeback.

Whatever one thinks of Baudrillard's analysis, we cannot avoid considering that the current reconfiguration of the relationship between communication and the political is also connected to this relationship between masses and images. What complicates matters is that, in a way, we cannot really say that the masses 'see' images. To see something (unlike to watch or to look) implies some kind of residual social qualities and we have determined that as long as we constitute a mass, whether we like it or not, or even if we resist it, we have none. Neither can we really talk about a 'mass perspective', in as much as the idea of perspective implies a subject which surveys and organizes, and traditionally the mass has always been described as a passive, 'feminine' entity. The notion of the mass implies a kind of distracted perception, of the kind, for example, that Walter Benjamin associated with architecture and the age of mechanical reproduction. The mass, that is, represents not so much a sociological perspective that identifies it with a specific class or class composition, as a relationship with the image. By all accounts, the relationship to the image that is expressed by the mass is one of fascination, that is a perception that deprives images of fixed qualities in order to amplify their intensities. Images are not so much decoded for meaning as consumed, that is absorbed and relayed. What the mass perceives in the image is its excess power of holding the gaze in fascination. As we have seen, we cannot really assimilate the mass to a historical subject in its modern sense. The way in which we have used this term here is to explain a certain relationship to images and media culture that constitutes a problem, for example, for the way we think about the politics of communication. If the masses are what within society resist the social, what resist mediation by relating to images in ways that neutralize their social qualities and meanings, then this is not a subject on which reason really takes hold. The masses imply a distracted perception that can be related to only as such – that is, as perception. It is only in so much as the masses perceive that their material composition and political disposition can be affected. Rational debates and communicative action have a marginal effect on this dynamic of fascination and distracted perception that we associate with mass culture.

This centrality of the relationship between perception and distraction within mass culture is recognized by communication managers and experts. Among the techniques and fields of expertise included in the area, for example, we count 'perception management'. The term was first coined within military and intelligence circles (the CIA under the directorship of William J. Casey) [12] but it is also expanding in the commercial sector with the emergence of perception management consultancy firms (interestingly enough many of them located in the Islamic world).[13] Perception management includes public relations work, knowledge of local conditions, information warfare and media manipulation, but in ways that explicitly recognize that what needs to be managed is not simply the knowledge that surrounds a certain event, but its 'perception'. Perception management is thus not mainly addressed to what we might recognize as a 'public opinion'. Although it does make some concessions to public opinion, it does not address it as a public that is able to discriminate between true and false and develop an informed position on this basis. In this sense, perception management belongs to the order of simulation. There is no scandal, but everything is more or less performed in the light (it is an obscene form of power, as Baudrillard remarked). What is important is not to convince public opinion of a truth that is demonstrated on the basis of logical arguments as the manipulation of an informational milieu. Images are not representations, but types of bioweapons that must be developed and deployed on the basis of a knowledge of the overall informational ecology. If the relationship between masses and images is characterized by the erasure of social qualities from the image, then all we are left with is not just a mass, but a universe of images, acting and reacting on each other – an artificial informational ecology of image flows. Like Henri Bergson, perception management too starts from the notion that perception is, first of all, in the images.

Seen from this perspective, it is not surprising that the most significant feature of contemporary mediascapes is their over-saturation with image and information flows (including the acoustic image or sound). To all effects these flows form a hyperreality or a cybernetic space, where images act and react on each other, giving rise to phenomena of parasitism, overcrowding, local image niches, underground micro-ecologies and so on. Thus, for example, one could analyse the image ecologies of global media culture by asking what is the rate of distribution of images in different locales; what kind of images achieve a kind of global dominance and which others are kept locally confined; what kind of networks organize different image flows and how these networks relate to each other; what characterizes a successful image and what happens to images that are not selected for mass diffusion; which images reinforce each other, which ones must be kept separate, which ones wage war on each other and so on.

When perceived by a mass, therefore, the universe of images seems to be *more* rather than *less* material. It is not a question of the media universe coming to constitute a map that replaces the real (as Baudrillard claimed, to think in terms of images as a copy of the real is to hark back to representation). It is more as if the universe of images has ceased to play the game of appearances and mediation to be openly displayed as a field for the propagation of intensities or affects – a battlefield for the war staged on the terrain of perception. What is important of an image, in fact, is not simply what it indexes – that is, to what social and cultural processes and significations it refers. What seems to matter is the kind of affect that it packs, the movements that it receives, inhibits and/or transmits. The place of an image is thus always within an ecology, not only because images derive their meanings from the overall semiotic system, but also because literally they act and react on each other – they wage war on each other or establish alliances (the bin Laden vs. Bush duets of the Afghan War; suicide bombers in city centres and army tanks in refugee camps; images of starvation side by side with images of conspicuous consumption); they find niches in which to proliferate and mutate (forgotten conspiracy theorists' fanzines and websites; idiosyncratic sexual fetishes); they infiltrate alien image environments and disrupt them by introducing new types of intensities (the graffitied trains delivering hip-hop intensity from Brooklyn into the heart of Manhattan in the late 1970s). This is the sense in which the hyperreal does not really involve a metaphysics of being and appearance so much as a kind of information ecology which also includes a dimension of warfare – a warfare to determine the differential power and dominance of some types of images over others. It is no longer a matter of illusion or deception, but of the tactical and strategic deployment of the *power of affection* of images as such. It is no longer a matter of truth and appearance, or even of the alienating power of the spectacle as 'opium of the masses', but of images as *bioweapons,* let loose into the informational ecology with a mission to infect.

If this world could appear to some as a world where appearances or spectacles have triumphed over reality, this is only because of a metaphysical prejudice that needs images to uphold the value of a truth that must always be uncovered. But is there anything that it is really left uncovered and secret within a distributed culture of communication? Is our problem really that media propaganda is used to cover up the truth? Or is it more the case that the truth is not even covered up any more because what is important is not to shield people from the truth but to have an effective strategy that is able to capture and hold together a certain type of intensity?

From this point of view, the emergence of a mass, of social entropy, always implies an intensification of communication strategies that focus on the intensity of the image and the afterlife that such intensities carry. The context of the first elaboration of theories of mass culture was notoriously that of twentieth-century totalitarian regimes for which the aesthetic management of perception was a key political technique (as the Frankfurt School theorists noticed and described). For Deleuze and Guattari, the totalitarian experiences of the twentieth century have also taught us about the power of one type of image over others – the face or the machine of faciality. Not only does the emergence of mass culture within modernity coincide with the rise of a star system that gravitates around a fascination with faces, but fascism as well (understood as a configuration of desire giving rise to authoritarian political systems) is inconceivable without the hegemony of a face. Within the ecology of images, faces play an important role and some faces become veritable black holes of social energies that are sunk into the empty space linking the eyes to the mouth. In this sense, George Orwell's Big Brother was about a surveillance society as much as it was about the imperialism of the face – the interplay of the eyes and mouth forming a closed circuit of communication in which the masses so to speak sink. Within the ecology of images, faces are like cluster nodes in the informational milieu and the succession of faces marks thresholds of passages and transformations in authoritarian political cultures (not only the iconic totalitarianism of Hitler, Mussolini, Stalin and Saddam Hussein, but also the populist authoritarianism of Ronald Reagan and Margaret Thatcher, the neo-imperialism of Tony Blair and George Bush, the theocratic pull of Osama bin Laden's face and so on).

But can we really reduce the relationship between communication and the political today to the perception of the masses – a pure perception that frees images of their socio-indexical anchorage in order to give free reign to an ecology of images understood as a propagation of intensity? Or wouldn't this be a reduction like that which says that all political communication is an appeal to reason? This does not mean to deny the existence either of a mechanism of formation of public opinion or of a relationship between images that are fundamentally ecological and microbiological. On the other hand, the mass culture or simulational hypothesis seems to overestimate the actual disappearance of the socio-indexical qualities of images in favour of a pure perception whereby images only act and react on each other. If on the one hand the configuration of the relationship between communication and the political that we call the masses indicates an important strategic target (involving a whole technology of perception management and information warfare), on the other hand this is not the whole story. A network culture, in fact, implies a complexification of the mass media environment – it is the dimension that envelops the multiple durations of disparate cultural formations and milieus. We are no longer in the mass-culture regime where the mass could be opposed on the one hand to a high culture of aesthetic discernment and reasonable debate and on the other to a folk culture that authentically expressed the power of the people. But neither can we oppose the TV masses to the Internet multitude without conveniently cutting out their intersections and relays in a common informational milieu. The image ecology of network culture is highly differentiated and this implies, *pace* Baudrillard, that images do not just flow through, but are channelled through a segmented and capillary system of communication. There is not simply an amorphous mass, but a fractal ecology of social niches and microniches. We are not living, that is, in a pure mass culture, but in a configuration of communication where a pure mass perception clashes and interacts with a fractured and microsegmented informational milieu.

AN INTOLERANT WORLD

As Armand Mattelart has pointed out, communication is a modern invention. It is modern, not because communication did not exist before the European eighteenth century, but rather because, as a term, communication belonged to another semiotic order. Emerging four centuries ago alongside the ideas of reason and progress, communication had older religious connotations of sharing, community, contiguity, incarnation and exhibition. In the 1753 entry to the *Encyclopédie* (one of the crowning achievements of the Enlightenment), the negative definition of communication explicitly points to the religious implications of the term.

> Written by a clergyman, it has the double merit of making us realize how much the original matrix of 'communication' owes to the language of the church while not being confined to it. Excommunication is defined in this article as the 'separation from communication or trade with a person with whom one previously enjoyed it... [any] man excluded from a society or a body, and with whom the members of that body no longer have communication, may be said to be excommunicated.[14]

This does not simply make today's 'socially excluded' the excommunicated of the information age, but also explains the affinity between religious sensibility and the universe of communication. We can only mention here the key function of communication in the production of a global community in the work of Marshall McLuhan – a converted Catholic;[15] and take in how Muslim thinkers immediately grasped the Internet in terms of its potential to produce an electronic Ummah.[16]

The early wave of theorization on the phenomenon of computer-mediated communication (CMC) also pointed to the importance of computer networks in the formation of 'virtual communities', as they became controversially known.[17] In spite of attempts to link them back to the pioneering times of the North American frontier, virtual communities looked more like the technological successors to the 'imagined communities' of modernity – including the national communities materialized by media events such as Franklin Delano Roosevelt's radio chats; presidential funerals and royal weddings; or films and TV series exploring the problems of a nation's history.[18]

The relationship between communication and community, which within modernity was mostly confined to the boundaries of the nation, is today problematized by a kind of geographical dispersion. Mediated communities are no longer mostly enclosed by national boundaries, but increasingly materialize at the intersection of manifold connections. Whether we are considering the multichannelled and multilingual universe of satellite television; or digitally encoded texts, images and sound on the Internet; or the visual icons of a global consumer culture devoted to brands and blockbuster action movies; or gossip and news relayed through phone calls and face-to-face communication – the nonlinear and distributed movement of information across a global communication matrix makes it hard to determine its relationship to a 'community' in the modern sense of the world.

The emergence of a global and differentiated communication matrix has also foregrounded the power of communication to *undo bonds,* rather than simply reinforce them – a feature that is particularly troubling for the modern association between communication and community. Referring to a comment by Abdel Monem Said on the inflammatory effects of images of the Palestinian Intifada on Arab youth, *New York Times* journalist George Packer was struck by how communication technologies (such as global television and Internet access) seem to have produced what he calls 'a world less tolerant'.[19]

From Marshall McLuhan to Ted Turner, Packer explains, media gurus have been predicting the emergence of a global village held together by a single communication infrastructure. Packer translates this to mean a world where information about human rights violations in the South would provoke the indignation of public opinion in the affluent North. Ideally, the resulting protests by indignant Western citizens would produce a synchronization of the planet on the values of the most 'advanced' societies – that is on the liberal values of tolerance, democracy and the recognition of fundamental human rights. Thus the communication of information about child labour in Thailand or Mexico would cause outrage in London and New York and this outrage would force politicians and corporations to change their policies. This was to be expected as the result of the formation of a global public opinion coinciding with the emergence of a global communication infrastructure. A smaller, more liberal world, then, would be a world where flagrant injustices could not be tolerated, and within which new international coalitions of activists, members of the public, and benevolent governments would gradually address global wrongs.

Cultural imperialism, always displayed a civilizing flair, but there is also another side to this failure of communication to pursue its supposedly civilizing mission. The failure of communication involves the crisis of the modern 'science of communicating', a science that Diderot in the same *Encyclopédie* article named 'rhetoric': the 'mode of understanding through reason'.[20] It is because the science of communicating is not simply that of understanding through reason that, for liberal public opinion, communication is making things worse. Who could have predicted that Third World youth would be driven to desire for *and* hatred of the West by the images beamed by Western sources to their TV sets and computer screens? Rather than providing fodder for indignation and reasons for action to citizens of the West, they are watching the media themselves and getting angry. Packer's examples are those of the Egyptian youth who want to become 'rock throwers' after seeing images of the Palestinian kids; and the Sierra Leonean teenager, who reportedly became a fighter because he was enraged by images of Western wealth and inflamed by American icons such as Rambo. Communication, the journalist concludes, is failing the world.

What the media provide is superficial familiarity – images without context, indignation without remedy. If the world seems to be growing more, rather than less, nasty these days, it might have something to do with the images all of us now carry around in our heads.[21]

Packer's article (and the long discussion that it engendered on the *slashdot* BBS immediately after its publication) is a good example of a recurring set of questions that are troubling the professionals of public opinion in relation to global communication. The notion that a more harmonic world would emerge out of better means of communication and open access to information and that this better world would lead to a progressive adaptation by 'backward' countries to advanced 'democratic' values has backfired. In the West, images of pain and suffering by citizens of less privileged countries reveal the limits of 'public opinion' actually to determine substantial political changes; in the South, disillusionment with Western cultural and political values produces widespread disenchantment and a return to ideas of religious purity.

How does the notion of an ecology of images compare to the thesis of communication as something that is making the world less tolerant? The answer to this question must be related somehow to the different dimensions that compose a network culture. A network culture is not a simple entity, but a composite and complex one: it includes a mass sensibility which characteristically deprives images of their socio-indexical qualities; a postmodern or late modern panache for fragmentation and difference; and a highly differentiated communication matrix in which images are continuously circulated, transformed and relayed at different times and across a variety of channels (Starsky and Hutch are always chasing villains somewhere in the mediascape ...). At this level, we have to acknowledge that even if images can no longer be considered primarily at the level of representation, they have not completely lost their indexical relationship to the social. Thus it would be hard to claim that there are no differences between images or that the differences of intensity that determine the relationship of images to each other have no relation to socially constructed meanings referring to specific socio-cultural segments. There are social and geopolitical reasons why Egyptian youth should react to images of the Palestinian Intifada the way they do. We thus do not simply have a mass, but also a fractured mass, and even a microsegmented one. The mass is not simply *massaged* by the medium, as Marshall McLuhan argued, but also *segmented* by the media. Image flows are not simply determined by the internal relationship between images as such, but also by the external relations that different images have with the social world.

This segmentation of the mass by way of the differentiation of image flows was summarized by Manuel Castells in his discussion of the sociological literature on 'the new media and the diversification of mass audience'. Castells identifies this mutation of the communication system with the diffusion of personal media devices such as the Sony Walkman, specialized radio, VCRs, and the explosion of cable and satellite television. Quoting Françoise Sabbah's assessment of new trends in the media in 1985, Castells acknowledges the enduring significance of her analysis for understanding contemporary cultural trends.

> In sum, the new media determine a segmented, differentiated audience that, although massive in terms of numbers, is no longer a mass audience in terms of simultaneity and uniformity of the message that it receives ... Because of the multiplicity of messages and sources, the audience itself becomes more selective. The targeted audience tends to choose its messages, so deepening its segmentation ...[22]

Image flows are thus no floating signifiers, but they work as material forces by virtue of their very differentials. They move at different speeds, have different paces, and their relationship with the world of solids is rather complicated. They do not just 'smooth' solids (as in pebbles or in the solid borders of national territories), but they sort them out (as rivers sort out different types of stone or as communication channels sort out different audiences).

An example of the complex relation linking these movements of segmentation to socio-cultural indexing is the emergence of what have been called 'migrant media'. Migrant media are media that cater specifically to the informational and cultural requests of the migrant communities that have coalesced all over the world as a result of widespread economic and political displacement of local populations. In a sense, that is, migrant media define all cultural consumption of media products that unify migrant communities across dispersed geographical spaces. Some of these migrant media have also caused a crisis within media activist circles, in as much as they seem to defy some of the tactics that worked well when the configuration of communication corresponded to a simple opposition between radical groups of anarchist or socialist disposition and the mainstream media as such. Tactical media activist and theorist David Garcia has given us an interesting example of the complexity inherent in the different speeds of image flows in a brief article on the relationship between mainstream media, tactical media and 'migrant media' in the Netherlands in the early years of the twenty-first century.

The background of the paper is the complex and overlapping arrangement of information flows and media systems in the Netherlands at the beginning of the twenty-first century (an arrangement that is both typical of countries of comparable wealth and atypical in as much as the Dutch context is marked by a particularly active grassroots media movement). The variety of communication networks that coexist in Amsterdam range from the world of mainstream media, including Dutch national media and international broadcasting (including French, German and British national television) to global media networks (from CNN to MTV and SKY); a thriving 'public access' cable television spearheaded by an active grassroots media movement of video producers and media activists; a high rate of Internet penetration, including the usual share of cybercafés and public access; and the whole network matrix of communication with which we are familiar (including intranets, telephony, wireless etc.). Rather than constituting a single communication space equally accessible to all parties concerned, this (a)typical network matrix is challenged, in Garcia's story, by the emergence of separate image flows, what he calls 'migrant media' – that is the increasing use by migrant communities of specific communication networks that do not overlap either with national or with global television.[23]

Garcia recounts how the progressive consolidation of such migrant media as self-enclosed islands catering to the needs of local migrant communities (and in particular Muslim communities) is implicated with the Dutch attitude to cultural differences (the epitome of liberalism in the West). Garcia suggests that in the Dutch model, differences are allowed to coexist, but only if they remain discrete and bounded, that is if they stay within their own confines. For Garcia, this situation underlines the development of the cultural and media milieu within the Dutch territory. On the one hand, a native population enjoying a more or less common media experience, that involves the consolidation of a national identity, but also of a specific experience of the global as mediated by the multinational media companies (such as CNN, Sky, BBC, etc.). On the other hand, the informai networks of migrant communities and local migrant media cable channels, with a strong presence of theocratic Islamic groups. In explaining the feedback loop between these separate media and cultural networks dividing migrant from native, the use by a theocratic Islamic group of public access cable TV and the emergence of an anti-immigrant Dutch right, Garcia recounts the confusion of the tactical media movement. While the latter started by advocating the necessity of public access to the media, it did not predict the formation of parallel media networks or that some of the forces taking over such networks would be so problematic from the point of view of a classic 'leftist' and 'new-leftist' politics.

It is not simply a matter here of showing how access to different media (let's say, to follow the Islam/West example, Al-Jazeera vs. CNN) produces different perspectives on issues such as the conflict between Israel and Palestine, or the Gulf War. As Packer argued, it is not just a matter of experience, but of what material relations of synchronization determine the dynamic emergence and becoming of national identities, migrant perspectives, emotions of solidarity and indignation, empathic identification and anger. This overall communication dynamics makes the world 'less tolerant' in as much as it aggravates the friction of differences that are both emphasized and left to rub off against each other outside of any mediation. This is why a network culture is not the United World of Benetton, where all differences are simply allowed to coexist and aesthetically enjoy each other. Communication networks latch onto the segmentation of the social, undermine *and* reinforce cultural identifications and release social antagonisms fed by shared experiences of injustice or indignation at imagined or real wrongs.

A network culture cannot thus be simply separated and opposed to the domain of the manipulated 'mass'. In as much as the dimension enveloped by a network culture crosses disparate domains of communication, it also seems to undercut and undermine even the volatile mass that occasionally lifts a pop icon, a TV format, or a brand logo out of the mostly flat input of the culture industry machine. There are thus mass phenomena within a network culture, but it is almost as if they always expressed only a dimension of the overall dynamics of communication. In a network culture, a mass is a transversal cut in the body of an informational milieu that never ceases to be microsegmented, highly differentiated and at the same time interconnected. If this mutual although uneven segmentation (where the masses segment and are segmented by the media) is possible at all, it is because differences have not simply become interchangeable, and social and cultural processes have not lost their capacity to qualify and differentiate image flows. At the same time, it has become necessary to think through the relationship between these social qualities and the mass perception identified above – we are always simultaneously *both* mass and class, mass *and* multitude, mass *and* race, mass *and* nation; and so on.

Psychoanalytic theory has of course spent a great deal of time analysing this relation, but mostly from the point of view of the individual subject rather than of the mass as such. Similarly, the old field of mass psychology developed according to very different modes of communication and was inflected by the political preoccupations of the time. Our starting point is not the problem of the 'revolutionary' or 'blind' masses, but the interplay between intensity and meaning as it takes place within a segmented mass. This interplay between intensity and meaning within an admittedly small mass (but a mass in a way has no size) has been recently described by Brian Massumi in 'The Autonomy of Affect'.[24] In his rereading of a behaviourist experiment on a group of children and their perception of different versions of a TV short (silent; with a matter-of-fact explanatory commentary; or with an emphatic and sentimental voice-over), Massumi shows that the affective perception of an image seems to be characterized by a gap. This gap is that between the *content* of the image (that is the social indexing or quality) and its *effect* (the strength or duration of the image, that is its intensity). In the experiment recounted by Massumi, the data produced by the electronic monitoring of the children's bodily reactions to different versions of the short film, and their stated reaction as articulated in their answers to the questionnaires, contradicted each other. Electrodes and questionnaires, the skin and the mouth, yielded different answers. Massumi argues that the experiment confirms the hypothesis of a gap between content and effect, a gap that results in a kind of 'autonomic remainder' of affect. In their collective response to the TV short, the children formed a 'mass', a bad conductor of meaning, but a fine conductor of intensities.

This gap between the social quality and the intensity of image perception is not simply a matter of sliding or floating signifiers, but is also about the autonomic potential of bodies and the chaotic dynamics of perception as an essential component of any cultural politics of communication. In the missing half-second between the moment when the skin reacts to the image and the moment when the brain registers the stimulus, all kinds of crossing of wires take place. The whole body is filled by the vibrations produced by the impact of images on sensory organs, including eyes, ears and skin. What we actually come to perceive consciously is only a fraction of what has touched us. In the movement from the first impact of perception to the moment of conscious elaboration, a whole chaotic dynamic unfolds, yielding extraordinarily stable results (social meanings consistent overall with the layout of social stratifications) but also pointing to the existence of autonomic bodily remainders, of unrealized, or virtual, potentials. This implies that the 'absorption of images' that characterizes the relationship between the masses and the media is far from being a simple process of manipulation and fascination.

If images are not the metaphysical cause of the corruption of communication, then we might have to consider them as the basic conditions within which a return of the political might take place. We might argue that the codes which organize media messages cannot be understood simply in terms of signification, that is as if the matter was simply that of manipulating a mass or mediating a meaning. Before such a capture of the image can be accomplished, a whole set of other operations must have taken place, operations that are both material and semiotic, but nevertheless microphysical. The power of communication and the media is not only the power of imposing an ideology, forming a consensus or manipulating the opinion of the majority, but also a *biopolitical power*, that is, a power of inducing perceptions *and* organizing the imagination, of establishing a subjective correspondence between images, percepts, affects and beliefs.[25] What appears challenging for cultural and media theory is that these flows of images/perceptions/sensations/intensities are not necessarily anchored in cultural and social identities narrowly conceived. Of course, this does not mean that people do not identify (with their race and gender, class and religion but also with celebrities and objects, pop stars and political leaders). These identifications qualify the images, but their social meanings do not completely capture the play of intensities – their autonomic remainder, as Massumi put it. It is this field of intensity that is invested by communication biopower, but, at the same time, this is also a site of emergence for *another* mode of politics that is not dependent on the modern problematic of communication. It is at this point, then, that we can return to our networked multitude: not as to a new subject rising to defy both the passivity of the mass and the corruption of communication, but as a *mass mutation* involving an experimentation with the zero degree of the political.

NETWORKED MULTITUDES

There is a mass, then, in network culture, as well as segments and microsegments, and an informational dimension that links them all. It is this peculiar feature of the overall communication system that a medium such as the Internet captures with uncanny fidelity. As in network culture at large, there is a mass psychology of the Net, unfolding, as Geert Lovink put it, within 'large-scale systems, filled with amorphous, more or less anonymous user masses'.[26] There are mass phenomena such as portal sites, the big search engines and free email services, but also the entertainment giants and the corporate news providers. At the same time, the segmentation of the audience that is observable in the new media landscape of satellite and local TV, or VCRs and DVDs, is replicated and intensified by the Internet – with its thousands of specialized web channels catering for niche audiences, but also with its myriad little electronic soapboxes with zero or so traffic and its firewalled networks and pushy newsletters. The concentration of portals, that is, does not preclude a high level of microsegmentation of usage across the dust-like galaxies of minor and specialized nodes. At the same time, however, this separation can never really neutralize the interconnectedness of the whole space, the overall vulnerability to informational dynamics, chain reactions, viral infections, the pollution of spam, or the powerful ripples of nonlinear information flows (the forwarding of links, petitions, cries for help, group emails, warnings and bugs, postings, and so on).

The Internet, that is, seems to us to capture (and reinforce) a feature of network culture as a whole – the way it combines masses, segments and microsegments within a common informational dimension in which all points are potentially even if unevenly affected by all other points. Within the Internet medium, this peculiar combination of masses and segments does not produce a peaceful coexistence of two different modes (the amorphous majority massing somewhere to the middle of a Bell curve and the rigid segments produced by socio-cultural processes of stratification). In a network culture, the differentiating power of image flows achieves a kind of hydrodynamic status characterized by a local sensitivity to global conditions. Rather than being dispersed at the receiving ends only to re-emerge as survey fodder, a networked mass displays a kind of active power of differentiation. It is still a mass, but it cannot be made to form a stable majority around some kind of average quality or consensus. The segments have lost some of their rigidity (whether of social or cultural identity) under the recombinant assault of informational flows. The result seems to be a political field that cannot be made to unite under any single signifier (such as the working class) or even under a stable consensus; while at the same time it cannot really split off into separate segments with completely separate socio-cultural identities (even hybrid ones) – a space that is *common,* without being *homogeneous* or even *equal.* As such, the Internet gives visibility to a larger feature of our communication milieu – and one that is on its way to becoming hegemonic, as all communication systems become ever more interconnected.

There is nothing idyllic about this political configuration. As a political milieu, a network culture looks more like a permanent battlefield than like a neo-socialist utopia. It is the plane over which battles for market shares and for the determination of public opinions are fought; it is a field of research into and deployment of advanced techniques and strategies of manipulation and control; it is the theatre of violent attacks and group hatreds. And yet, it also offers plenty of opportunities for experimentation with political tactics and forms of organization. This experimentation addresses both the dimension of an overall informational dynamics (that is the necessity to develop informational tactics able to counteract the overbearing power of corporate and governmental actors in the communication sectors); and also a political and cultural milieu that can no longer be subsumed (if it ever was) under a majority, led by a class/avant-garde/idea or even made to form a consensus that is not inherently fractured and always explosively unstable.

The recent movements against the neoliberal policies of the great international economic bodies such as the International Monetary Fund (IMF), the World Bank, the World Trade Organization (WTO) and the group of the eight most powerful economies in the world (the G8); the Social Forum meetings assembling an international movement of mayors, political parties, NGOs, indigenous groups, media activists and others (from Porto Alegre, Brazil 2000 to Mumbai, India 2004); the anti-war coalitions giving rise to the global demos against the Second Gulf War in February 2003; these are all examples of such experimentation (and of the potentials and problems that are inherent in such a process). All these events have given temporary, but powerful visibility to a process of horizontal and diffuse communication that draws both upon the latest technologies (from video cellular telephony to wireless Internet access) and also upon more established strategies, such as conferences, talks, camps, workshops, meetings and travelling caravans (such as in the preparation of the 1998/2000 anti-IFM, G8 and WTO demos).[27] These multiple modes of communication correspond to a mostly uncoordinated proliferation of organizations, micro-organizations and groups, with more or less shifting boundaries, but with common interests and, most importantly, operating within a common communication matrix.

As a result, these first years of the twenty-first century have consistently displaced the familiar opposition of the political spectrum (inherited from the cold war) between left and right. What has displaced them, however, is neither the fetish of difference (as in post-1960s social movements) nor that of public opinion as a new superpower, but a more general compossibility of relations within a fluid and yet segmented bio-informational milieu. In this sense, the encounter between the spectacle and politics suggested by Baudrillard opens up onto challenging scenarios. If the degree zero of politics, as Sylvère Lotringer put it in a different context, is related to 'the desire to allow differences to deepen at the base without synthesizing them from above, to stress similar attitudes without imposing a general line, to allow points to co-exist side by side', then this desire is tested by a communicational milieu that demands it *pragmatically* rather than simply discursively or ideologically.[28]

Theorists of network politics have repeatedly pointed out how this impossibility of building a consensus or stable forms of organization is a key resource (rather than a limit) of its political potential. For Hardt and Negri, a network culture constitutes a new occasion for the re-emergence of the multitude – a political category that they oppose to the preconstituted unity of a 'people' (the multitude is 'a multiplicity, a plane of singularities, an open set of relations, which is not homogeneous or identical with itself and bears an indistinct, inclusive relation to those outside of it....an inconclusive constituent relation...').[29] For the Critical Art Ensemble, the absence of a unitary purpose or shared meaning is an advantage:

> conflicts arising from the diversity of the cells would function as a strength rather than a weakness; this diversity would produce a dialogue between a variety of becomings that would resist

bureaucratic structures as well as provide a space for happy accidents and breakthrough inventions.[30]

For Harry Cleaver, computer-linked social movements form a 'hydrosphere', a fluid space 'changing constantly and only momentarily forming those solidified moments we call "organizations." Such moments are constantly eroded by the shifting currents surrounding them so that they are repeatedly melted back into the flow itself.'[31]

The virtual movements of this early twenty-first century have offered a challenging glimpse of the political field opened up by communication biopower. A network micropolitics able to traverse the global space of communication is not some kind of easy utopia, where differences are allowed to coexist or go their separate ways – the domain of a blissfully unproblematic self-organization. On the contrary, it is the ways in which the global communication matrix allows such connections and organizations to take place that reveals the hard work implied. This scattering, this tendency to diverge and separate, coupled with that of converging and joining, presents different possible lines of actualization: it can reproduce the rigid segments of the social and hence its ghettos, solipsisms and rigid territorialities. And it also offers the potential for a political experimentation, where the overall dynamics of a capillary communication milieu can be used productively as a kind of common ground – allowing relations of compossibility as well as concerted actions.

Within this context, a cultural politics of communication involves not simply the exercise of an abstract faculty of reason, but also a very material engagement with relations of composition and decomposition between affectively charged and often competing *beliefs*. Thus it cannot simply dismiss or despair at the state of the *mass*, that is, of those that reason believes to be misled and hoodwinked. What this ultimately boils down to is a capacity to synthesize not so much a common position (from which to win the masses over), but a common *passion* giving rise to a *distributed movement* able to displace the limits and terms within which the political constitution of the future is played out. What this effort starts with, however, is not Reason, in the sense of a universal faculty that, thanks to interactivity and a decentralized distribution of communication capabilities, finally resurfaces after a long slumber. As with the masses, this political mode cannot but start with affects – that is with intensities, variations of bodily powers that are expressed as fear and empathy, revulsion and attraction, sadness and joy. It does not see such affects as an aberration of communication (as the 'communication is making the world less tolerant' thesis would argue) but as their beginning – as expressing the zero degree of the political as such. It is a reason that cannot be moulded by an effort to transcend and regulate the body's affects (which was always implicit in the modernist politics of the avant garde, where the question was that of enlightening a mass). On the contrary, *it arises out* of affective investments and works through an inventive and emotive political intelligence on the terrain of the *common* – the constituent terrain of the contemporary politics of communication.[32]

Notes

INTRODUCTION

1. Virilio is referring here to Albert Einstein's famous statement in the 1950s that humanity would have to face three kinds of bombs: 'The first bomb, the atomic bomb, was manufactured in the United States during the Second World War and dropped on Hiroshima in Japan in 1945. The second bomb was the information bomb. The third bomb was the population bomb set to explode in the twenty-first century' (John Armitage in Paul Virilio and Friedrich Kittler 'The Information Bomb: a conversation', esp. p.81). In Virilio's reading, the information bomb is a 'technological and political weapon... largely the product of US-military and America-owned multinational firms' (ibid.). The effects of this bomb are 'the acceleration of world history and unprecedented technological convergence together with the appearance of "real time," the disappearance of physical space, and the rise of "technological fundamentalism," and "social cybernetics"' (ibid.).
2. Virilio and Kittler 'The Information Bomb', p. 85. See also Paul Virilio *The Information Bomb*.

CHAPTER 1

1. Friedrich A. Kittler 'A History of Communication Media'.
2. Ibid.
3. C.E. Shannon and W. Weaver *The Mathematical Theory of Communication*, p. 1.
4. Jérôme Segal, *Théorie de l'information*.
5. Norbert Wiener *Cybernetics*, p. 39.
6. Jeremy Campbell *Grammatical Man*, p. 17.
7. Jacob D. Bekenstein 'Information in the Holographic Universe', esp. p. 50.
8. Wiener *Cybernetics*, p. 39.
9. Claude E. Shannon 'A Mathematical Theory of Communication', esp. p. 5.
10. Warren Weaver 'Recent Contributions to the Mathematical Theory of Communication', in Shannon and Weaver *The Mathematical Theory of Communication*, p. 99.
11. F. J. Crasson 'Information Theory and Phenomenology', p. 100.
12. Ibid., p. 128.
13. Ibid., p. 129.
14. Michel Serres *Hermes: Literature, Science, Philosophy*, p. 67.
15. Serres *Hermes*, p. 67.
16. J. C. R. Licklider and Robert W. Taylor 'The computer as a communication device', p. 21.

17. Gilbert Simondon *L'individuation psychique et collective*.
18. See William Bogard 'Distraction and Digital Culture'.
19. Shannon 'A Mathematical Theory of Communication', p. 15.
20. Ibid., p. 11
21. Claude Shannon apparently stumbled on Ludwig Boltzmann's formula for entropy as an effective measure of information, but was very reluctant to use the two terms together or even use them at all (he had doubts about adopting the term information as such because of its use in common parlance; and entropy because of its controversially metaphysical status within the natural sciences). An anecdote suggests that it was John von Neumann who suggested that Shannon referred to entropy anyway. Von Neumann apparently convinced him that 'since nobody knows what entropy is, in a debate you will be sure to have an advantage' (quoted in Howard Rheingold, *Tools for Thought*, p. 125). This did not stop Shannon from decrying the abuse that he felt was directed towards information theory and the 'bandwagon effect' that, especially after Watson and Crick's claim in 1952 that they had cracked the genetic code, made information the next big thing after energy.
22. See Shannon and Weaver *The Mathematical Theory of Communication*, p. 100–1.
23. Wiener *Cybernetics*, pp. 10–11.
24. The example is taken from W. Ross Ashby *Introduction to Cybernetics*.
25. Weaver 'Recent Contributions', p. 100.
26. Wiener *Cybernetics*, p. 10.
27. Thus for Brian Massumi,

> [w]hat characterizes communication is that it is designed to be 'transparent': no conversion is supposed to take place by virtue of the connection in and of itself... information is a feed. Neutral packets ('data') are consumed on one side of the window (or screen) to feed a process already understood or under way, with known effect and intent. Nothing new... The connection is segregated from the conversion. (Brian Massumi 'Sensing the Virtual, Building the Insensible', p. 1081).

28. Marco d'Eramo 'L'abisso non sbadiglia più', p.29 (my translation).
29. See Henri Bergson *Matter and Memory*; Gilles Deleuze *Bergsonism*; and also Brian Massumi 'Sensing the Virtual, Building the Insensible'; and Pierre Lévy *Becoming Virtual*.
30. Shannon 'A Mathematical Theory of Communication', p. 20.
31. Fisher quoted in Jérôme Segal *Théorie de l'information* (my translation).
32. Campbell *Grammatical Man*, p. 39.
33. Ibid.
34. Ibid., p. 44.
35. See Luciana Parisi *Abstract Sex*.
36. Quoted in Armand Mattelart *The Invention of Communication*, p. 228.
37. See Scott Lash and John Urry *The End of Organized Capitalism*.
38. Norbert Wiener *The Human Use of Human Beings*, p. 64.
39. Ibid., p. 65.

40. Gregory Bateson *Mind and Nature*, p. 49.
41. Wiener *The Human Use of Human Beings*, p. 11.
42. Pierre Levy *Collective Intelligence*, p. 48
43. James Gleick 'Push Me Pull You'.
44. Michel Foucault's analysis of Velásquez's *Las Meninas* is still the best analysis of the relation between perspectival space, representation and the subject in modernity (in M. Foucault *The Order of Things*).
45. See Rodney Brooks *Flesh and Machines*.

CHAPTER 2

1. Antonio Negri 'On Gilles Deleuze and Felix Guattari, *A Thousand Plateaus*', p. 1188.
2. See http://www.swatch.com/fs_index.php?haupt=itime&unter= (last accessed 12 March 2003).
3. Beyond Swatch, the two other virtual times quoted by Lovink are the open source venture, XTime and the art project TIMEZONE. See Geert Lovink *Dark Fiber*, esp. p. 143.
4. Lovink *Dark Fiber* p. 142.
5. See David Holmes *Virtual Globalization*.
6. Michael Hardt and Antonio Negri *Empire*.
7. Joseph Stiglitz has described the 'Washington consensus' that ruled the economic governance of globalization as a kind of 'market fundamentalism' (see Joseph Stiglitz *Globalization and Its Discontents*).
8. Manuel Castells *The Rise of the Network Society*, p. 398.
9. See Paul Virilio *The Information Bomb*.
10. A threat to the navigability of the Internet is constituted by 'alternate roots', that is, domain spaces that are not approved by ICANN or even the Internet Architecture Board. The threat of such domains is that of a fragmentation of network space, in as much as being located on a competing grid would impact on how accessible a document is. On the problem of 'alternate roots', see 'The Domain Name System: A Non-Technical Explanation – Why Universal Resolvability Is Important', *InterNic*, http://www.internic.net/faqs/authoritative-dns.html (last updated 25 Mar 2002; last accessed 10 April 2002).
11. On ICANN and the problems inherent in Internet governance, see Stefaan Verhulst 'Public legitimacy: ICANN at the crossroads'.
12. On the relationship between net art and the corporate Internet, see also Josephine Berry, 'The Thematics of Site-Specific Art on the Net'.
13. Tim Berners-Lee *Weaving the Web*, p. 128.
14. On the vectorial dynamics of global communication spaces see Mackenzie Wark *Virtual Geography*.
15. See Duncan J. Watts *Small Worlds*; and Albert-László Barabási *Linked*.
16. See Barabási *Linked*, pp. 166–7.
17. See Ien Ang 'Global Media/Local Meanings'; and also George Ritzer *The McDonaldization of Society*.
18. On this subject, see Keith Ansell Pearson and John Mullarkey 'Introduction', in *Henry Bergson: Key Writings*.

19. Gilles Deleuze *Cinema 1: The Movement-Image*, p. 11.
20. Gregory Bateson *Mind and Nature*, p. 174.
21. Reliable statistics about email traffic are notoriously difficult to acquire. However, we have access to some other data such as spam statistics which offer at least a glimpse of the sheer scale of overall email traffic. The Korean Information Security Agency, for example, has estimated that in 2002 alone, the number of spam messages received by Korean email users on a daily basis was about 915 million. The annual figure was 333.9 billion. (See Korean Information Security Agency ' Spam causes W2.6 tril. in damage a year', http://www.kisa.or.kr/english/trend/2002/trend_20020501_01.html [last accessed 17 June 2003].)
22. See Barabási *Linked*.
23. See Janet Abbate *Inventing the Internet*.
24. 'Celebrating the Birthday of the Internet January 1, 1983, the Cutover from NCP to TCP/IP', *Telepolis*, http://www.heise.de/tp/english/inhalt/te/14017/1.html (last accessed 28 January 2003). Thanks to Ronda Hauben for signalling this on the *nettime* list.
25. On content censorship in authoritarian regimes see Shanthi Kalathil and Taylor C. Boas 'The Internet and State Control in Authoritarian Regimes'.
26. Thirty years later, with the routine use of Computer Assisted Design in architectural practice, something of the very same pliability and dynamism of space would make its way back into the world of non-electronic space; see Brian Massumi 'Sensing the Virtual, Building the Insensible'.
27. Network Working Group (ed. B. Carpenter) 'Architectural Principles of the Internet'.
28. Stephen Segaller *Nerds 2.0.1*, p. 22.
29. Abbate *Inventing the Internet*, p. 51.
30. Ibid., p. 128.
31. Antonio Negri has made this shift from the mass worker to immaterial labour as the centre of growth a cornerstone of his understanding of the shifting terrain of political antagonism in the post-1970s period. As is well known, he has argued that immaterial labour implies a shift from 'economicist' (or quantitative) understanding of value to a *biopolitical model* (addressing the active powers of cooperation of the many). (On this subject see Antonio Negri *Guide*.)
32. Berners-Lee *Weaving the Web*, p. 14.
33. Abbate *Inventing the Internet*, p. 48.
34. Berners-Lee *Weaving the Web*, p. 15.
35. Hardt and Negri *Empire*, p. 166.
36. Ibid., p. 167.
37. Ibid., p. 112.
38. As usual, technological breakthroughs are characterized by multiple points of emergence. Thus the principles of a packet-switched network were also outlined by a British engineer, Donald Davies, at the British National Physics Laboratory; he had come up with a similar idea for communication between computers (see Segaller *Nerds 2.0.1*).
39. Network Working Group 'Architectural Principles of the Internet'.

40. Ibid.
41. Paul Baran 'On Distributed Communications'.
42. See David Tetzlaff 'Yo-Ho-Ho and a Server of Warez'.
43. Sociologists of the Internet have already pointed out some of the social reasons for this feature of the Internet, such as the early constituency of computer scientists and engineers. On the relation between Internet architecture and social groups, see Tim Jordan *Cyberpower*; and also Manuel Castells *The Internet Galaxy*.
44. See Rebecca Blood 'Weblogs'.
45. See Phil Agre on the entropic dangers of mailing lists in 'Subject: Avoiding heat death on the Internet'.
46. See Geert Lovink 'The Moderation Question: Nettime and the Boundaries of Mailing List Culture', in *Dark Fiber*, pp. 68–121.
47. See Allucquère Rosanne Stone 'Will the Real Body Please Stand Up?'
48. Inke Arns and Andreas Broeckmann 'Rise and Decline of the Syndicate'.
49. Agre 'Subject: Avoiding heat death on the Internet'.
50. On this subject, see Richard W. Wiggins' account of the effect of 11 September on Google (Richard W. Wiggins 'The Effects of September 11 on the Leading Search Engine'), for an account of the propagation of news about the disaster, see also Michael Blakemore and Roger Longhorn 'Communicating Information about the World Trade Center Disaster'.

CHAPTER 3

1. This chapter has been made possible by research carried out with the support of the 'Virtual Society?' programme of the Economic and Social Research Council (ESRC) (grant no. L132251050). I shared this grant with Sally Wyatt and Graham Thomas, Department of Innovation Studies, University of East London. The chapter has previously been published as 'Free Labor: producing culture for the digital economy' in *Social Text* volume 18, number 2 (2000), pp. 33–58
2. See Andrew Ross's ethnography of NYC digital design company Razorfish, *No-Collar*.
3. http://www.disobey.com/netslaves/. See also Bill Lessard and Steve Baldwin's playful classification of the dot-com labour hierarchies in *Net Slaves*.
4. Lisa Margonelli 'Inside AOL's 'Cyber-Sweatshop'', p. 138.
5. See Paolo Virno and Michael Hardt *Radical Thought in Italy*; and Toni Negri *The Politics of Subversion* and *Marx Beyond Marx*.
6. Negri *The Politics of Subversion*.
7. Donna Haraway *Simians, Cyborgs, and Women*, p. 159.
8. Paul Gilroy *The Black Atlantic*, p. 40.
9. Manuel Castells*The Rise of the Network Society*, p. 395.
10. Antonio Negri *Guide*, p. 209 (my translation).
11. In discussing these developments, I will also draw on debates circulating across Internet sites such as *nettime*, *Telepolis*, *Rhizome* and *Ctheory*. Online debates are one of the manifestations of the surplus value engendered

by the digital economy, a hyperproduction which can only be partly reabsorbed by capital.

12. Ross *No-Collar*, p. 9.
13. See Richard Barbrook 'The Digital Economy'; and 'The High-Tech Gift Economy'. See also Anonymous 'The Digital Artisan Manifesto'; and Andrew Ross's argument that the digital artisan was an expression of a short-lived phase in the Internet labour market corresponding to a temporary shortage of skills that initially prevented a more industrial division of labour (Andrew Ross *No-Collar*).
14. Barbrook 'The High-Tech Gift Economy', p. 135.
15. Ibid., p. 137
16. Don Tapscott *The Digital Economy*, p. xiii.
17. Ibid., p. 35 (my emphasis).
18. Ibid., p. 48.
19. For a discussion of the independent music industry and its relation with corporate culture, see David Hesmondalgh 'Indie'. Angela McRobbie has also studied a similar phenomenon in the fashion and design industry in *British Fashion Design*.
20. See the challenging section on work in the high-tech industry in Josephine Bosma et al. *Readme!Filtered by Nettime*.
21. Martin Kenney 'Value-Creation in the Late Twentieth Century: The Rise of the Knowledge Worker', in Jim Davis et al. (eds) *Cutting Edge: Technology, Information Capitalism and Social Revolution*; in the same anthology see also Tessa Morris-Suzuki 'Capitalism in the Computer Age'.
22. See Darko Suvin 'On Gibson and Cyberpunk SF', in *Storming the Reality Studio*, ed. Larry McCaffery (London and Durham: Duke University Press, 1991), 349–65; and Stanley Aronowitz and William Di Fazio *The Jobless Future*. According to Andrew Clement, information technologies were introduced as extensions of Taylorist techniques of scientific management to middle-level, rather than clerical, employees. Such technologies responded to a managerial need for efficient ways to manage intellectual labour. Clement, however, seems to connect this scientific management to the workstation, while he is ready to admit that personal computers introduce an element of autonomy much disliked by management (Andrew Clement 'Office Automation and the Technical Control of Information Workers').
23. Barbrook 'The High-Tech Gift Economy'.
24. See Kevin Robins 'Cyberspace or the World We Live In'.
25. See Frank Webster *Theories of the Information Society*.
26. Maurizio Lazzarato (1996) 'Immaterial Labor' in Saree Makdisi et al. (eds) *Marxism Beyond Marxism*, p. 133.
27. The Criminal Justice Act was popularly perceived as an anti-rave legislation and most of the campaign against it was organized around the 'right to party'. However, the most devastating effects of the CJA have struck the neo-tribal, nomadic camps, basically decimated or forced to move to Ireland in the process. See Andrea Natella and Serena Tinari, eds, *Rave Off*.
28. Maurizio Lazzarato 'Immaterial Labor', p. 136.

29. In the two volumes of *Capitalism and Schizophrenia*, Gilles Deleuze and Felix Guattari described the process by which capital unsettles and resettles bodies and cultures as a movement of 'decoding' ruled by 'axiomatization'. Decoding is the process through which older cultural limits are displaced and removed as with older, local cultures during modernization; the flows of culture and capital unleashed by the decoding are then channelled into a process of axiomatization, an abstract moment of conversion into money and profit. The decoding forces of global capitalism have then opened up the possibilities of immaterial labour. See Gilles Deleuze and Felix Guattari *Anti-Oedipus*; and *A Thousand Plateaus*.

30. See Franco Berardi (Bifo) *La Nefasta Utopia di Potere Operaio*, p. 43.

31. See Kevin Kelly *Out of Control*.

32. Eugene Provenzo 'Foreword', in Pierre Levy *Collective Intelligence*, p. viii.

33. Pierre Levy *Collective Intelligence*, p. 13.

34. Ibid., p. 1.

35. See Little Red Henski 'Insider Report from UUNET' in Bosma et al. *Readme! Filtered by Nettime*, pp. 189–91.

36. Paolo Virno 'Notes on the General Intellect' in Makdisi et al. (eds) *Marxism Beyond Marxism*, p. 266.

37. Karl Marx *Grundrisse*, p. 693.

38. Paolo Virno 'Notes on the General Intellect', p. 266.

39. Ibid., p. 270.

40. Ibid., p. 271

41. See Maurizio Lazzarato 'New Forms of Production' in Bosma et al. *Readme! Filtered by Nettime*, pp. 159–66; and Tessa Morris-Suzuki 'Robots and Capitalism' in Davis et al. (eds) *Cutting Edge*, pp. 13–27.

42. See Toni Negri 'Back to the Future' in Bosma et al. *Readme! Filtered by Nettime*, pp. 181–6; and Donna Haraway *Simians, Cyborgs, Women*.

43. Andrew Ross *Real Love*.

44. See Richard Barbrook 'The High-Tech Gift Economy'.

45. The work of Jean-François Lyotard in *The Postmodern Condition* is mainly concerned with *knowledge,* rather than intellectual labour, but still provides a useful conceptualization of the reorganization of labour within the productive structures of late capitalism.

46. See Arthur Kroker and Michael A. Weinstein *Data Trash*.

47. See Howard Rheingold *The Virtual Community*.

48. See Howard Rheingold 'My experience with Electric Minds' in Bosma et al. *Readme! Filtered by Nettime*, pp. 147–50; also David Hudson *Rewired*. The expansion of the Net is based on different types of producers adopting different strategies of income generation: some might be using more traditional types of financial support (grants, divisions of the public sector, in-house Internet divisions within traditional media companies, business web pages which are paid for like traditional forms of advertising) or by generating interest in one's page and then selling the user's profile or advertising space (freelance web production); or by innovative strategies of valorization such as book publishing (e-commerce).

49. See Margonelli 'Inside AOL's "Cyber-Sweatshop"'.

50. Andrew Leonard 'Open Season', p. 140. Open source harks back to the specific competencies embodied by Internet users in its pre-1994 days. When most net users were computer experts, the software structure of the medium was developed by way of a continuous interaction of different technical skills. This tradition still survives in institutions like the Internet Engineering Task Force (IETF), which is responsible for a number of important decisions about the technical infrastructure of the Net. Although the IETF is subordinated to a number of professional committees, it has important responsibilities and is open to anybody who wants to join. The freeware movement has a long tradition, but it has also recently been divided by the polemics between the free software or 'copyleft' movement and the open-source movement, which is more of a pragmatic attempt to make freeware a business proposition (see debates on www.gnu.org; www.salonmag.com).

51. Andrew Leonard 'Open Season'.

52. Ibid., p. 142

53. It is an established pattern of the computer industry, in fact, that you might have to give away your product if you want to reap the benefits later on. As John Perry Barlow has remarked, '[F]amiliarity is an important asset in the world of information. It may often be the case that the best thing you can do to raise demand for your product is to give it away' (John Perry Barlow 'Selling Wine Without Bottles', p. 23). Apple started it by giving free computers to schools, an action which did not determine, but certainly influenced the subsequent stubborn presence of Apple computers within education; MS-DOS came free with IBM computers.

54.
> ... the technical and social structure of the Net has been developed to encourage open cooperation among its participants. As an everyday activity, users are building the system together. Engaged in 'interactive creativity', they send emails, take part in listservers, contribute to newsgroups, participate within on-line conferences and produce websites (Tim Berners-Lee, 'Realising the Full Potential of the Web' <http//www.w3.org//1998/02/Potential.html>). Lacking copyright protection, information can be freely adapted to suit the users' needs. Within the hi-tech gift economy, people successfully work together through '...an open social process involving evaluation, comparison and collaboration'. (Richard Barbrook 'The High-Tech Gift Economy', pp. 135–6).

55. John Horvarth 'Freeware Capitalism', posted to *nettime*, 5 February 1998.

56. Ibid.

57. Netscape started like a lot of other computer companies: its founder, Marc Andreessen, was part of the original research group which developed the structure of the World Wide Web at the CERN laboratory, in Geneva. As with many succesful computer entrepreneurs, he developed the browser as an offshoot of the original, state-funded research and soon started his own company. Netscape was also the first company to exceed the economic limits of the computer industry, in as much as it was the

first successful company to set up shop on the Net itself. As such, Netscape exemplifies some of the problems which even the computer industry met on the Net and constitutes a good starting point to assess some of the common claims about the digital economy.

58. Andrew Ross *Real Love*.
59. Chip Bayers 'Push Comes to Show', p. 113.
60. Ibid., p. 156
61. Ibid.

CHAPTER 4

1. Lewis Mumford *Technics and Civilization*, p. 163.
2. On the artificiality of the plane of nature, see Luciana Parisi's discussion of molecular biology in *Abstract Sex*.
3. See Kevin Kelly *Out of Control*.
4. Christopher G. Langton 'Artificial Life', in C. G. Langton (ed.) *Artificial Life*, p. 5.
5. Charles Taylor and David Jefferson 'Artificial Life as a Tool for Biological Inquiry', p. 1.
6. Manuel De Landa, drawing on the scientific literature on the subject, has summarized this shift as from the 'ideal type' to the 'population'. The concept of the 'ideal type' is of Aristotelian origin and dominated biological thought for over 2000 years. In the concept of the 'ideal type', 'a given population of animals was conceived as being the more or less imperfect incarnation of an ideal essence'. We can understand the notion of 'ideal type' also according to the principles of semiotics, where each sign is composed of a 'signifier' (in De Landa's example the word 'zebra') that refers to a 'signified' (the 'ideal' zebra conceived as possessing all the essential features of zebrahood). All real zebras (the referent in Saussurian terminology) are therefore specific and necessarily imperfect incarnations of the ideal type 'zebra' that constitutes the signified or concept underlying the noun. The revolution introduced by 'population thinking' in the 1930s (and a necessary moment in the production of the current biological turn) is thus that the ideal type (or we could say, the sign) is abandoned for the population. At the centre of evolutionary theory we do not find any longer an ideal animal, made up of all those traits that allowed it to evolve and survive in a specific environment, but a set of differentiated traits, spread across all the population of all zebras, a relatively stable system crossed by continuous variation. The new object of evolutionary theory, then, is not the fit individual but the dynamic of populations. (Manuel De Landa 'Virtual Environments and the Emergence of Synthetic Reason').
7. John H. Holland *Emergence*, p. 88.
8. See Rodney Brooks *Flesh and Machines*.
9. Gregory Bateson *Steps to an Ecology of Mind*, p. 288.
10. Kevin Kelly *Out of Control*, pp. 16–18.
11. Langton 'Artificial Life', p. 3.
12. Ibid., p. 6.

13. George A. Cowan 'Conference Opening Remarks' in Cowan et al. (eds) *Complexity*, p. 3.
14. Homa Baharami and Stuart Evans 'Flexible Recycling and High-Technology Entrepreneurship', in Martin Kenney (ed.) *Understanding Silicon Valley*, p. 166.
15. Holland *Emergence*, p. 113.
16. Manuel Castells and Peter Hall *Technopoles of the World*.
17. Kelly *Out of Control*, p. 13.
18. Holland *Emergence*, p. 241.
19. Kelly *Out of Control*, p. 21.
20. *Ibid.*, p. 12.
21. Atomic theory, a pre-Socratic suggestion, claims that the universe is composed of all the possible combinations of tiny invisible and indivisible elements called 'atoms' falling freely through an unbounded and void space. As Lucretius, the author of the Epicurean poem–treatise *De Rerum Natura*, or *On the Nature of the Universe*, put it: '*When the atoms are travelling straight down through empty space by their own weight, at quite indeterminable times and places they swerve ever so little from their course,* just so much that you can call it a change of direction. If it were not for this swerve [clinamen], everything would fall downwards like raindrops through the abyss of space. No collision would take place and no impact of atom upon atom would be created. Thus nature would never have created anything.' (Lucretius *On the Nature of the Universe*, p. 43.
22. Ilya Prigogine and Isabelle Stengers *Order Out of Chaos*, p. 141.
23. Michel Serres *Hermes: Literature, Science, Philosophy*, p. 100.
24. Steven Levy *Artificial Life*, p. 109.
25. Tim Berners-Lee *Weaving the Web*, p. 203.
26. Prigogine and Stengers *Order out of Chaos*, p. 14.
27. Manuel De Landa 'Deleuze and the Use of the Genetic Algorithm in Architecture'.
28. See Manuel De Landa, 'Virtual Environments'.
29. Duncan J. Watts *Small Worlds*, p. 181.
30. Mark Ward *Virtual Organisms*, p. 78.
31. See Brian Massumi 'Chaos in the "total field" of vision', in *Parables for the Virtual*.
32. See George Caffentzis 'Why Machines Cannot Create Value', in J. Davis et al. (eds) *Cutting Edge*, pp. 29–56.
33. See Watts *Small Worlds*, p. 186.
34. Ibid.
35. One of the ambitions of CA researchers, in fact, is not simply to build an abstract machine able to overcome the limits of the Turing machine, but also that of modelling the *logic of life*. It is life, in fact, that is imagined as a great computational machine able to program matter and hence to engender the wide variety of forms that evolution has produced on earth. In particular, by taking on the perspective of *populations* (in this case populations of cells or particles), CA researchers aspire to copy the mechanical capacity of evolutionary dynamics to *invent* new forms of life. Artificial life scientists in particular are very keen to point out that there is no vitalism at stake here. They do not believe that life is a mysterious quality

able to produce living beings. On the contrary, as Langton remarked, the understanding of evolutionary dynamics in place in ALife is strictly mechanistic (although nondeterministic). Life is no mysterious quality that descends from above to the earth, but an emergent process that results from the interaction of a multitude of elements in relations of local connection. (See Langton 'Artificial Life'.)

36. Lev Manovitch *The Language of New Media*, p. 213.
37. Kelly *Out of Control*, p. 27.
38. Luc Steel 'Emergence Functionality in Robotic Agents through on-line evolution' in Rodney A. Brooks. and Pattie Maes (eds) *Artificial Life IV*, p. 8
39. Cariani, Peter 'Emergence and Artificial Life', in C. G. Langton, et al. (eds) *Artificial Life II*, p. 775.
40. See the Bionomics Institute site at http://www.bionomics.org/text/insttute/sop.html (last accessed 15 August 2000).
41. Sadie Plant 'The Virtual Complexity of Culture', p. 206.
42. Quoted in Howard Rheingold *The Virtual Community*, p. 7.
43. Ibid.
44. Nicholas Negroponte *Being Digital*, p. 181
45. Taylor and Jefferson 'Artificial Life', p. 8.
46. Stefan Helmreich *Silicon Second Nature*, p. 47.
47. Richard Dawkins *The Selfish Gene*, p. 29.
48. Ibid., p. 26
49. Ibid., p. 34
50. Ibid., p. 35.
51. Gilles Deleuze *Negotiations*.
52. On this subject see Andrew Ross *The Chicago Gangster Theory of Life*.
53. Franco Berardi (Bifo) *La fabbrica dell'infelicitá*.
54. Franco Berardi 'Social Entropy and Recombination', p. 20.

CHAPTER 5

1. Joseph Stiglitz *Globalization and Its Discontents*, p. 229.
2. On this subject, see Armand Mattelart *The Invention of Communication*.
3. For an influential critique of this notion of communication, see Jacques Derrida 'Signature, Event, Context', in P. Kamuf (ed) *A Derrida Reader*.
4. See Jürgen Habermas 'The Public Sphere', p. 102.
5. Ibid.
6. See John Hartley *The Politics of Pictures*. For a discussion of cyberdemocracy, the Internet and the public sphere see also Mark Poster 'Cyberdemocracy'.
7. On this subject, see Timothy Bewes 'Truth and appearance in politics: the mythology of spin', in T. Bewes and J. Gilbert *Cultural Capitalism*, pp. 158–76.
8. Jean Baudrillard *In the Shadow of the Silent Majorities*, p. 46.
9. See John Cassidy *Dot.con*.
10. See autonome a.f.r.i.k.a.-gruppe, Luther Blissettt and Sonja Bruenzels 'What about Communication Guerrilla? A message about guerilla

communication out of the deeper German backwoods', Version 2.0, posted to *nettime*, 16 September 1998 (available at http://amsterdam. nettime.org/Lists-Archives/nettime-l-9809/msg00044.html; last accessed 23 June 2003).

11. Jean Baudrillard *In the Shadow*, p. 37.

12. See Robert Parry 'Lost History'.

13. For an example, see Mediators, a Pakistan-based firm of perception management consultancy, http://www.praffairs.com/perception.htm, whose clients include Microsoft and Shell Pakistan.

14. Armand Mattelart *The Invention of Communication*, p. xiii.

15. See Arthur Kroker 'Digital Humanism: The Processed World of Marshall McLuhan', in Arthur and Marilouise Kroker (eds) *Digital Delirium*.

16. See Gary Bunt *Virtually Islamic*.

17. See Howard Rheingold, *The Virtual Community*. For a sample of the polemic that greeted Howard Rheingold's book see also Kevin Robins 'Cyberspace or the World We Live In'.

18. On the subject of communication, community and nationalism, see Benedict Anderson *Imagined Communities*; and also Paddy Scannell *Radio, Television, and Modern Life*.

19. George Packer 'Where Here Sees There'.

20. Mattelart, *Intervention*, p. xiii.

21. Packer 'Where Here Sees There'; see also the 'Communication Making the World Less Tolerant' thread at http://slashdot.org/article. pl?sid=02/04/21/1238236.

22. Quoted in Manuel Castells *The Rise of the Network Society*, pp. 339–40.

23. David Garcia 'Islam and Tactical Media on Amsterdam Cable', posted to *nettime*, 3 April 2002 (available at http://amsterdam.nettime.org/Lists-Archives/nettime-l-0204/msg00018.html).

24. Brian Massumi *Parables for the Virtual*.

25. To interrogate the relationship between images, affects and ideas involves an assessment of the relationship between bodies and minds, ethics and morality. From this perspective, it is useful to remember Gilles Deleuze's 'morality test', which suggests that we follow a simple method for defining the difference between an ethical and a moralistic perspective on the world. Whenever you have an opposition of interests and tendencies between body and soul, there you have the moral law. Wherever you think that the body's needs and desires are directly opposed to and in contrast with those of the consciousness/mind/soul, there you have an ignorance of the power of the body and hence an emerging morality (see Gilles Deleuze *Expressionism in Philosophy*).

26. Geert Lovink *Dark Fiber*, esp. p. 137.

27. See Tiziana Terranova 'Demonstrating the globe: virtual and real action in the network society' in D. Holmes (ed.) *Virtual Globalization*.

28. Sylvère Lotringer and Christian Marazzi (eds) *Italy*.

29. Michael Hardt and Antonio Negri *Empire*, p. 103.

30. Critical Art Ensemble 'Electronic Civil Disobedience, Simulation, and the Public Sphere'; see also their pamphlet *Electronic Civil Disobedience and other unpopular ideas*.

31. Cleaver prefers the notion of a 'hydrosphere' to that of the net in as much as the latter seems to him to be more appropriate to global organizations such as the NGOs that rely on stable nodes organized with a view to act on specific issues. Network-based movements, on the other hand, seem to him to exceed the network because of the intrinsic mobility of their elements, connected together by a multiplicity of communication channels, converging and diverging in mobile configurations. Harry M. Cleaver 'Computer-linked Social Movements and the Global Threat to Capitalism'. On forms of agency in networked environments, see also Andreas Broeckmann 'Minor Media – Heterogenic Machines'.

32. It was a pre-Enlightenment materialist thinker, Baruch Spinoza, who convincingly spoke of the importance of affects and passions as the basic terrain of politics; and it was again Spinoza who considered the production of common notions as the basic process through which the ethical constitution of the world takes place. On this subject, see Benedictus de Spinoza *The Collected Work of Spinoza*. See also Antonio Negri *The Savage Anomaly*; and Moira Gatens *Imaginary Bodies*.

Bibliography

Abbate, Janet *Inventing the Internet* (Cambridge, Mass.: MIT Press, 1999)

Agre, Phil 'Subject: Avoiding heat death on the Internet', in J. Bosma et al. (eds) *Readme! Filtered by Nettime* (New York: Autonomedia, 1999), pp. 343–56

Anderson, Benedict *Imagined Communities: reflections on the origin and spread of nationalism* (London: Verso, 1991, second edition)

Ang, Ien 'Global Media/Local Meanings', in *Living Room Wars: Rethinking Media Audiences for a Postmodern World* (London and New York: Routledge, 1996)

Anonymous 'The Digital Artisan Manifesto', posted to *nettime*, 15 May 1997

Arns, Inke and Andreas Broeckmann 'Rise and Decline of the Syndicate: the End of an Imagined Community', posted to nettime-l@bbs.thing.net, 13 November 2001

Aronowitz, Stanley and William Di Fazio *The Jobless Future: Sci-Tech and the Dogma of Work* (Minneapolis and London: University of Minnesota Press, 1994)

Ashby, W. Ross *An Introduction to Cybernetics* (London: Chapman & Hall, 1957)

Barabási, Albert-László *Linked: The New Science of Networks* (Cambridge, Mass.: Perseus Publishing, 2002)

Baran, Paul 'On Distributed Communications ' (Memorandum RM-3420-PR), August 1964, Rand Corporation, http://www.rand.org/publications/RM/RM3420/ (last accessed 15 May 2003)

Barbrook, Richard 'The High-Tech Gift Economy', in Josephine Bosma et al. *Readme! Filtered by Nettime: ASCII Culture and the Revenge of Knowledge* (New York: Autonomedia, 1999), pp. 132–8

—— 'The Digital Economy', posted to *nettime*, 17 June 1997 (also at www.nettime.org)

Barlow, John Perry 'Selling Wine Without Bottles: the Economy of Mind on the Global Net', in Peter Ludow (ed.) *High Noon on the Electronic Frontier: Conceptual Issues in Cyberspace* (Cambridge, Mass.: MIT Press, 1996)

Bateson, Gregory *Mind and Nature: A Necessary Unity* (New York: E. P. Dutton, 1979)

—— *Steps to an Ecology of Mind* (St. Albans: Paladin, 1973)

Baudrillard, Jean *In the Shadow of the Silent Majorities* (New York: Semiotext(e), 1983)

Bayers, Chip 'Push Comes to Show', *Wired*, volume 7, number 2 (February 1999), p. 113

Bekenstein, Jacob D. 'Information in the Holographic Universe', *Scientific American*, August 2003, pp. 48–55

Berardi, Franco 'Social Entropy and Recombination' in *ØYES make-world* paper no. 2 (November 2002) (translated by Erik Simpson and Arianna Bo), p. 20

—— *La Nefasta Utopia di Potere Operaio* (Roma: Castelvecchi/DeriveApprodi, 1998)

—— *La fabbrica dell'infelicitá. New Economy e movimento del cognitariato* (Roma: DeriveApprodi, 2001)

Bergson, Henri *Matter and Memory* (translated by N. M. Paul and W. S. Palmer) (New York: Zone Books, 1988)

Berners-Lee, Tim *Weaving the Web: The Original Design and Ultimate Destiny of the World Wide Web* (New York: Harper Business, 2000)

—— 'Realising the Full Potential of the Web', http//www.w3.org//1998/02/Potential.html (last accessed 2 February 2003)

Berry, Josephine, 'The Thematics of Site-Specific Art on the Net' (unpublished Ph.D. thesis), University of Manchester, 2001

Bewes, Timothy and Jeremy Gilbert (eds) *Cultural Capitalism: Politics After New Labour* (London: Lawrence & Wishart, 2000)

Blakemore, Michael and Roger Longhorn 'Communicating Information about the World Trade Center Disaster: Ripples, Reverberations, and Repercussions', *First Monday*, volume 6, number 12 (December 2001), http://firstmonday.org/issues/issue6_12/blakemore/index.html (last accessed 22 August 2003)

Blood, Rebecca 'Weblogs: a history and perspective', *Rebecca's pocket*, http://www.rebeccablood.net/essays/weblog_history.html (last updated September 2000; last accessed 22 April 2003)

Bogard, William 'Distraction and Digital Culture', *Ctheory*, Articles: A088, 10 May 2000, http://www.ctheory.net/text_file.asp?pick=131 (last accessed 21 August 2003)

Bosma, Josephine, Pauline Van Mourik Broekmann, Ted Byfield, Matthew Fuller, Geert Lovink, Diana McCarty, Pit Schultz, Felix Stalder, McKenzie Wark and Faith Wilding *Readme! Filtered by Nettime: ASCII Culture and the Revenge of Knowledge* (New York: Autonomedia, 1999)

Broeckmann, Andreas 'Minor Media – Heterogenic Machines', posted to nettime-l@Desk.nl, 13 November 1998 (also at http://www.nettime.org/Lists-Archives/nettime-l-9811/msg00029.html; last accessed 23 June 2003)

Brooks, Rodney *Flesh and Machines: How Robots Will Change Us* (New York: Vintage Books, 2002)

Brooks, Rodney A. and Pattie Maes (eds) *Artificial Life IV: Proceedings of the Fourth International Workshop on the Synthesis and Simulation of Living Systems* (Cambridge, Mass: MIT Press, 1995)

Bunt, Gary *Virtually Islamic: Computer-mediated Communication and Cyber Islamic Environments* (Cardiff: University of Wales Press, 2000)

Campbell, Jeremy *Grammatical Man: Information, Entropy, Language, and Life* (New York: Simon & Schuster, 1982)

Cassidy, John *Dot.con: The Greatest Story Ever Sold* (London: Penguin Press, 2002)

Castells, Manuel *The Internet Galaxy: reflections on the internet, business, and society* (Oxford: Oxford University Press, 2001)

—— *The Rise of the Network Society* (Oxford: Blackwell, 1996)

Castells, Manuel and Peter Hall *Technopoles of the World: The making of 21st Century Industrial Complexes* (London and New York: Routledge, 1994)

Clement, Andrew 'Office Automation and the Technical Control of Information Workers' in Vincent Mosco and Janet Wasko (eds) *The Political Economy of Information* (University of Wisconsin Press, 1988)

Cleaver, Harry M. 'Computer-linked Social Movements and the Global Threat to Capitalism', posted to aut-op-sy@lists.village.virginia.edu, 11 December 1999 (also at http://www.cseweb.org.uk/downloads/cleaver.pdf)

Clough, Patricia Ticineto *Autoaffection : unconscious thought in the age of teletechnology* (Minneapolis: University of Minnesota Press, 2000)

Cowan, George A., David Pines and David Meltzer (eds) *Complexity: Metaphors, Models, and Reality*, Proceedings Vol. XIX, Santa Fe Institute, Studies in the Sciences of Complexity (Reading, Mass.: Addison-Wesley Publishing Company, 1994), pp. 1–3

Crasson , F. J. 'Information Theory and Phenomenology', in Crasson and Sayre (eds) *Philosophy and Cybernetics* (University of Notre Dame Press, 1967)

Critical Art Ensemble 'Electronic Civil Disobedience, Simulation, and the Public Sphere', posted to nettime-l@Desk.nl, 11 January 1999

—— *Electronic Civil Disobedience and Other Unpopular Ideas* (New York: Autonomedia, 1996)

Davis, Jim, Thomas Hirsch and Michael Stack (eds) *Cutting Edge: Technology, Information, Capitalism and Social Revolution* (London: Verso, 1997)

Dawkins, Richard *The Selfish Gene* (New York: Oxford University Press, 1976)

De Landa, Manuel 'Deleuze and the Use of the Genetic Algorithm in Architecture', http://boo.mi2.hr/~ognjen/tekst/delanda2001.html (last accessed 21 June 2003)

—— 'Virtual Environments and the Emergence of Synthetic Reason', http://www.t0.or.at/delanda.htm (1998; last accessed 20 May 2002)

Deleuze, Gilles *Bergsonism* (New York: Zone, 1988)

—— *Cinema 1: The Movement-Image* (London: Athlone Press, 1992), p. 11

—— *Expressionism in Philosophy: Spinoza* (New York: Urzone, 1990)

—— *Negotiations: 1972–1990* (New York: Columbia University Press, 1995)

Deleuze, Gilles and Felix Guattari *A Thousand Plateaus: Capitalism and Schizophrenia* (London: Athlone Press, 1988)

—— *Anti-Oedipus: Capitalism and Schizophrenia* (London: Athlone Press, 1984)

d'Eramo, Marco 'L'abisso non sbadiglia più', in G. Baglione, F. Carlini, S. Carrà, M. Cini, M. d'Eramo, G. Parisi and S. Ruffo (eds) *Gli Ordini del Caos* (Roma: Manifesto Libri, 1991), pp. 19–70

Foucault, Michel *The Order of Things: An Archaeology of the Human Sciences* (London and New York: Routledge, 1992 [1970])

Garcia, David 'Islam and Tactical Media on Amsterdam Cable', posted to *nettime*, 3 April 2002 also at http://amsterdam.nettime.org/Lists-Archives/nettime-l-0204/msg00018.html)

Gatens, Moira *Imaginary Bodies: ethics, power and corporeality* (London, Routledge, 1996)

Gilroy, Paul *The Black Atlantic: Modernity and Double Consciousness* (London and New York: Verso, 1993), p. 40

Gleick, James 'Push Me Pull You', *New York Times Magazine*, 23 March 1997 (also at http://www.around.com/push.html, last accessed 23 June 2003)

—— *Chaos* (Abacus, 1987)

Habermas, Jürgen 'The Public Sphere: An Encyclopedia Article', in Meenakshi Gigi Durham and Douglas M. Kellner (eds) *Media and Cultural Studies: Keyworks* (Oxford: Blackwell, 2001, pp. 102–7), p. 102

Hall, Stuart 'Encoding, Decoding', in Simon During (ed.) *Cultural Studies: A Reader* (London and New York: Routledge, 1993), pp. 90–103

Haraway, Donna *Simians, Cyborgs, and Women: The Reinvention of Nature* (London: FA Books, 1991)

Hardt, Michael and Antonio Negri *Empire* (Harvard University Press, 2000)

Hartley, John *The Politics of Pictures: The Creation of the Public in the Age of Popular Media* (New York: Routledge, 1992)

Helmreich, Stefan *Silicon Second Nature: Culturing Artificial Life in a Digital World* (Berkeley, Los Angeles, London: University of California Press, 2000)

Hesmondalgh, David 'Indie: The Aesthetics and Institutional Politics of a Popular Music Genre', *Cultural Studies* volume 13, number 1 (January 1999), pp. 34–61

Holland, John H. *Emergence: From Chaos to Order* (Cambridge, Mass.: Perseus Books, 1998)

Holmes, David (ed.) *Virtual Globalization: Virtual Spaces/Tourist Spaces* (London and New York: Routledge, 2000)

Hudson, David *Rewired: a brief (and opinionated) net history* (Indianapolis: Macmillan Technical Publishing, 1997)

Jordan, Tim *Cyberpower: the culture and politics of cyberspace and the Internet* (London: Routledge, 1999)

Kalathil, Shanthi and Taylor C. Boas 'The Internet and State Control in Authoritarian Regimes: China, Cuba, and the Counterrevolution', *First Monday*, volume 6, number 8 (August 2001), http://firstmonday.org/issues/issue6_8/kalathil/index.html; (last accessed 16 June 2003)

Kamuf, Peggy (ed.) *A Derrida Reader: Between the Blinds* (New York: Columbia University Press, 1991)

Kelly, Kevin *Out of Control: The New Biology of Machines, Social Systems, and the Economic World* (Reading, Mass.: Addison-Wesley, 1994)

Kenney, Martin (ed.) *Understanding Silicon Valley: The Anatomy of an Entrepreneurial Region* (Stanford, Calif.: Stanford University Press, 2000)

Kittler, Friedrich 'A History of Communication Media', *Ctheory*, 30 July 1996, http://www.ctheory.net/text_file.asp?pick=45 (last accessed 21 August 2003)

Kroker, Arthur and Marilouise (eds) *Digital Delirium* (New York: St. Martin's Press, 1997)

Kroker, Arthur and Michael A. Weinstein *Data Trash: the Theory of the Virtual Class* (New York: St. Martin's Press, 1994)

Langton, Christopher G. (ed.) *Artificial Life: The Proceedings of an Interdisciplinary Workshop on the Synthesis and Simulation of Living Systems Held September*

1987 in Los Alamos, New Mexico, Vol. VI (Redwood City, Calif.: Addison Wesley, 1989)

Langton, Christopher G., Charles Taylor, J. Doyne Farmer, Steen Rasmussen (eds) *Artificial Life II: Proceedings of the Workshop on Artificial Life Held February 1990 in Santa Fe, New Mexico*, Proceedings Vol. X, Santa Fe Institute, Studies in the Sciences of Complexity (Redwood City, Calif.: Addison Wesley, 1992)

Lash, Scott *Critique of Information* (London: Sage, 2002)

Lash, Scott and John Urry *The End of Organized Capitalism* (Cambridge: Polity Press, 1987)

Lazzarato, Maurizio 'Immaterial Labor', in Saree Makdisi et al. (eds) *Marxism Beyond Marxism* (London: Routledge, 1996)

Leonard, Andrew 'Open Season', *Wired*, volume 7, number 5 (May 1999)

Lessard, Bill and Steve Baldwin *NetSlaves: True Tales of Working the Web* (New York: McGraw Hill, 2000)

Levy, Pierre *Becoming Virtual: Reality in the Digital Age* (translated by Robert Bononno) (New York and London: Plenum Trade, 1988)

—— *Collective Intelligence: Mankind's Emergent World in Cyberspace* (Cambridge, Mass.: Perseus Books, 1999)

Levy, Steven *Artificial Life: A Report from the Frontier where Computers meet Biology* (New York: Vintage Books, 1992)

Licklider, J. C. R. and Robert W. Taylor 'The computer as a communication device', in *In Memoriam: J. C. R. Licklider 1915–1990* (Palo Alto: CA Systems Research Centre, 1990)

Lotringer, Sylvère and Christian Marazzi (eds) *Italy: Autonomia: Post-Political Politics* (New York: Semiotext(e), 1980)

Lovink, Geert *Dark Fiber: Tracking Critical Internet Culture* (Cambridge, Mass. and London, England: MIT Press, 2002)

Lucretius *On the Nature of the Universe* (translated by R. E. Latham; revisions, introduction and notes by John Godwin) (London: Penguin Books, 1994)

Lyotard, Jean-François *The Postmodern Condition: A Report on Knowledge* (translated by Geoff Bennington and Brian Massumi) (Minneapolis: University of Minnesota Press, 1989)

McCaffery, Larry (ed.) *Storming the Reality Studio* (London and Durham: Duke University Press, 1991)

McRobbie, Angela *British Fashion Design: Rag Trade or Image Industry?* (London and New York: Routledge, 1998)

Makdisi, Saree, Cesare Casarino and Rebecca E. Karl (eds) (for the *Polygraph* collective) *Marxism Beyond Marxism* (London: Routledge, 1996)

Manovitch, Lev *The Language of New Media* (Cambridge, Mass.: MIT Press, 2001)

Margonelli, Lisa 'Inside AOL's "Cyber-Sweatshop"', *Wired*, volume 7, number 10 (October 1999), p. 138

Marx, Karl *Grundrisse* (London: Penguin Books, 1973)

Massumi, Brian 'Sensing the Virtual, Building the Insensible', in Gary Genosko (ed.) *Deleuze and Guattari: Critical Assessments of Leading Philosophers* (London and New York: Routledge, 2001)

—— *Parables for the Virtual: Movement, Affect, Sensation* (Durham and London: Duke University Press, 2002)

Mattelart, Armand *The Invention of Communication* (Minneapolis: University of Minnesota Press, 1996)

Mumford, Lewis *Technics and Civilization* (London: George Routledge and Sons, 1934)

Natella, Andrea and Serena Tinari (eds) *Rave Off* (Roma: Castelvecchi, 1996)

Negri, Antonio 'On Gilles Deleuze and Felix Guattari, *A Thousand Plateaus*', in G. Genosko (ed.) *Deleuze and Guattari* (London and New York: Routledge, 2001)

—— *Guide. Cinque Lezioni su* Impero *e dintorni* (Milano: Raffaello Cortina Editore, 2003)

—— *Marx Beyond Marx: Lessons on the* Grundrisse (New York: Autonomedia, 1991)

—— *The Politics of Subversion: A Manifesto for the Twenty-First Century* (Cambridge: Polity Press, 1989)

—— *The Savage Anomaly: The Power of Spinoza's Metaphysics and Politics* (translated by Michael Hardt) (Minneapolis and Oxford: University of Minnesota Press, 1991)

Negroponte, Nicholas *Being Digital* (New York: Alfred A. Knopf, 1995)

Network Working Group (ed. B. Carpenter) 'Architectural Principles of the Internet', http://www.ietf.org/rfc/rfc1958.txt June 1996; last accessed 16 June 2003)

Packer, George 'Where Here Sees There' *New York Times*, 21 April 2002, http://www.nytimes.com/2002/04/21/magazine/21WWLN.html?ex=1051070400&en=82a6368b52165a3b&ei=5070. (last accessed 1 December 2002)

Parisi, Luciana *Abstract Sex: Philosophy, Biotechnology and the Mutations of Desire* (London: Continuum Press, 2004)

Parry, Robert 'Lost History: CIA perception management', *Consortium*, http://www.consortiumnews.com/archive/lost12.html (accessed 8 June 2003)

Pearson, Keith Ansell and John Mullarkey 'Introduction', in *Henry Bergson: Key Writings* (London and New York: Continuum, 2002), pp. 1–45

Plant, Sadie 'The Virtual Complexity of Culture', in G. Robertson et al. *FutureNatural* (London and New York: Routledge, 1996), pp. 203–17

Poster, Mark 'Cyberdemocracy: The Internet and the Public Sphere', in David Porter (ed.) *Internet Culture* (New York and London: Routledge, 1997), pp. 201–18.

Prigogine, Ilya and Isabelle Stengers *Order Out of Chaos: Man's New Dialogue with Nature* (Toronto, New York, London and Sidney: Bantam Books, 1984)

Rheingold, Howard *The Virtual Community: Homesteading on the Electronic Frontier* (Harper Perennials, 1994)

—— *Tools for Thought: The History and Future of Mind-Expanding Technology* (Cambridge, Mass: MIT Press, 2000 [1985])

Ritzer, George *The McDonaldization of Society* (Thousand Oaks, Calif. : Pine Forge Press, 2000)

Robins, Kevin 'Cyberspace or the World We Live In', in Jon Dovey (ed.) *Fractal Media: New Media in Social Context* (London: Lawrence & Wishart, 1996)

Ross, Andrew *No-Collar : the humane workplace and its hidden costs* (New York: Basic Books, 2003)

—— *Real Love: In Pursuit of Cultural Justice* (London and New York: Routledge, 1998)

—— *The Chicago Gangster Theory of Life* (London and New York: Verso, 1994)

Scannell, Paddy *Radio, Television, and Modern Life: a phenomenological approach* (Oxford : Blackwell, 1996)

Segal, Jérôme *Théorie de l'information : sciences, techniques et société de la seconde guerre mondiale à l'aube du XXIe siècle* (Thèse de Doctorat, Faculté d'Histoire de l'Université Lyon II, Chaire Interuniversitaire d'Histoire des Sciences et des Techniques, 1988), http://www.mpiwg-berlin.mpg.de/staff/segal/thesis/ (last accessed 7 October 2003)

Segaller, Stephen *Nerds 2.0.1.: A Brief History of the Internet* (New York: TV Books LLC, 1998)

Serres, Michel *Hermes: Literature, Science, Philosophy* (edited by Josue V. Harari and David F. Bell) (Baltimore and London: Johns Hopkins University Press, 1982)

Severin, Werner and James Tankard *Communication Theories* (fourth edition) (New York: Longman, 1997), p. 47

Shannon, Claude E. 'A Mathematical Theory of Communication', in N.J.A. Sloane and Aaron D. Wyner (eds) *Claude Elwood Shannon Collected Papers* (New York: IEEE Press, 1999), pp. 5–83

Shannon, Claude E. and Warren Weaver *The Mathematical Theory of Communication* (Indiana: Universiy of Illinois Press, 1963 [1949])

Simondon, Gilbert *L'individuation psychique et collective. À la lumiére des notions de Forme, Information, Potentiel et Métastabilité* (Paris: Editions Aubier, 1989)

Spinoza, Benedictus de *The Collected Work of Spinoza* (Princeton, N.J.: Princeton University Press, 1985)

Stiglitz, Joseph *Globalization and Its Discontents* (London: Penguin Books, 2002)

Stone, Allucquère Rosanne 'Will the Real Body Please Stand Up? Boundary stories about virtual cultures', in D. Bell and B.M. Kennedy (eds) *The Cybercultures Reader* (London and New York, Routledge, 2000), pp. 504–28

Suvin, Darko 'On Gibson and Cyberpunk SF', in Larry McCaffery (ed.) *Storming the Reality Studio* (London and Durham: Duke University Press) pp. 349–65

Tapscott, Don *The Digital Economy* (New York: McGraw Hill, 1996)

Taylor, Charles and David Jefferson 'Artificial Life as a Tool for Biological Inquiry', in C.G. Langton (ed.) *Artificial Life: An Overview* (Cambridge, Mass.: MIT Press, 1995, pp. 1–13)

Tetzlaff, David 'Yo-Ho-Ho and a Server of Warez: Internet Software Piracy and the New Global Information Economy', in A. Herman and T. Swiss (eds) *The World Wide Web and Contemporary Cultural Theory* (London and New York : Routledge, 2000), pp. 99–126

Verhulst, Stefaan 'Public legitimacy: ICANN at the crossroads', *Open Democracy*, http://www.opendemocracy.net/forum/document_details.asp?CatID=18& DocID=611&DebateID=109 (September 2001)

Virilio, Paul *The Information Bomb* (translated by Chris Turner) (London and New York: Verso, 2000)

Virilio, Paul and Friedrich Kittler 'The Information Bomb: a conversation', *Angelaki: journal of the theoretical humanities* (special issue *Machinic Modulations, New Cultural Theory and Technopolitics*) volume 4, number 2 (September 1999), pp. 81–90

Virno, Paolo and Michael Hardt *Radical Thought in Italy: A Potential Politics* (Minneapolis: University of Minnesota Press, 1996)

Ward, Mark *Virtual Organisms: The Startling World of Artificial Life* (London: Macmillan, 1995)

Wark, Mackenzie *Virtual Geography: Living With Global Media Events* (Bloomington: Indiana University Press, 1994)

Watts, Duncan J. *Small Worlds: The Dynamics of Networks between Order and Randomness* (Princeton, NJ.: Princeton University Press, 1999)

Weaver, Warren 'Recent Contributions to the Mathematical Theory of Communication', in C.E. Shannon and W. Weaver *The Mathematical Theory of Communication* (Urbana: University of Illinois Press, 1963 [1949])

Webster, Frank *Theories of the Information Society* (London and New York: Routledge, 1995)

Wiener, Norbert *Cybernetics or Control and Communication in the Animal and the Machine* (Cambridge, Mass.: MIT Press, 1961)

—— *The Human Use of Human Beings: Cybernetics and Society* (London: FA Books, 1989).

Wiggins, Richard W. 'The Effects of September 11 on the Leading Search Engine', *First Monday,* volume 7, number 10 (October 2001), http://firstmonday.org/issues/issue6_10/wiggins/index.html (last accessed 22 August 2003)

Index